SAT & ACT Vocabulary Workbook #1

ISBN: 979-8-89480-850-5

To our family –
Love you for all you do!

This book belongs to

_____

_____

_____

Table of Contents

Table of Contents

How to Use this Book

1

CONSISTENT PRACTICE

Aim to learn 20 new words each week to steadily build your vocabulary.

2

ENGAGE WITH THE MATERIAL

Take your time with each activity, ensuring you understand the meaning and usage of each word.

3

STAY MOTIVATED

Keep track of your progress and celebrate your improvements as you go through the workbook.

4

EXPAND YOUR KNOWLEDGE

The word meanings provided are not exhaustive, and some words can have multiple meanings. Use the references to continue expanding your vocabulary.

How to Use this Book

 ## Match

- Start with the word list provided.
- Use the word bank to match each vocabulary word with its correct meaning.
- Familiarize yourself with the words and their definitions.

 ## Unscramble

- Move on to the word scramble section.
- Unscramble the letters to form the correct vocabulary words
- Reinforce your memory and understanding of the words.

 ## Search

- Use the unscrambled words to complete the word search puzzle.
- Find these words within the grid to further reinforce your recognition and recall abilities.

 ## Crossword

- Use the crossword clues to fill in the crossword puzzle.
- Each clue corresponds to a vocabulary word from the word bank.
- Test your understanding of the words in context and improve your problem-solving skills.

 ## Word Bank

- Remember, all puzzles use only the words in the word bank.
- If you get stuck, flip back and use the word bank to help you find the correct answers.

 ## Check

- Answers to all the puzzles are provided at the end of the book.
- Use these to check your work and ensure you understand each word correctly.

Word List #1

1. _____ Reverent or devout outwardly

2. _____ Wordy

3. _____ Recognize or perceive differences

4. _____ Excessively confident

5. _____ Easily controlled

6. _____ To feel or express sorrow

7. _____ To agree without protesting

8. _____ To forcibly restrict

9. _____ To glorify

10. _____ Huge and powerful entity

Acquiesce	Constrain	Futile	Replete
Antagonist	Convention	Insurgent	Slight
Austere	Deplore	Pedestrian	Timorous
Behemoth	Discriminate	Pertinacious	Tractable
Bombastic	Exalt	Pious	Verbose

Word List #1

11. _____ One who rebels

12. _____ Stubbornly persistent

13. _____ Filled or well-supplied

14 _____ An insult or a very small amount

15. _____ Opposes the protagonist

16. _____ An assembly of people

17. _____ Timid

18. _____ Very bare

19. _____ Producing no result or effect

20. _____ Lacking inspiration or dull

Acquiesce	Constrain	Futile	Replete
Antagonist	Convention	Insurgent	Slight
Austere	Deplore	Pedestrian	Timorous
Behemoth	Discriminate	Pertinacious	Tractable
Bombastic	Exalt	Pious	Verbose

Word Scramble #1

1. ACDEIIIMNRST   D _____
2. AEERSTU   A _____
3. ACCEEIQSU   A _____
4. BEEHHMOT   B _____
5. GHILST   S _____
6. EFILTU   F _____
7. AAGINNOSTT   A _____
8. BEEORSV   V _____
9. CEINNNOOTV   C _____
10. AELTX   E _____
11. IMOORSTU   T _____
12. EGINNRSTU   I _____
13. ACEIINOPRSTU   P _____
14. ACINNORST   C _____
15. DEELOPR   D _____
16. EEELPRT   R _____
17. ADEEINPRST   P _____
18. AABCELRTT   T _____
19. IOPSU   P _____
20. ABBCIMOST   B _____

Word Search #1

```
Z A N T A G O N I S T Z N R
J C A E N S R X C J X P H U
X Q N B B R E P L E T E K V
S U B O X I L S J G Q D L Z
D I S C R I M I N A T E N C
C E H C Q G H B B L Q S B K
H S C O N H S L I G H T I Y
G C O N S S D E P L O R E E
H E N S B O M B A S T I C L
C M V T E R S V I L H A Q K
K I E R H F S P Q X V N U I
T N N A E G T I K N M A X K
B S T I M O R O U S I J T G
I U I N O U A U S T E R E Q
F R O D T O C S O G S A X J
L G N A H X T H O R A L A Y
P E R T I N A C I O U S L K
K N A B O Z B Q V K H C T Y
W T F U T I L E D C K C L T
G F B B G V E R B O S E A C
```

Crossword Clues #1

Across

1. Huge and powerful entity
7. To agree without protesting
10. Lacking inspiration or dull
12. To forcibly restrict
14. To glorify
17. Filled or well-supplied
18. Stubbornly persistent
19. Wordy

Down

1. Excessively confident
2. Producing no result or effect
3. Reverent or devout outwardly
4. Recognize or perceive differences
5. Opposes the protagonist
6. An insult or a very small amount
8. An assembly of people
9. Easily controlled
11. One who rebels
13. Very bare
15. Timid
16. To feel or express sorrow

Crossword Puzzle #1

Word List #2

1. _____ Supposed or assumed true

2. _____ A particular moral excellence

3. _____ Calmness

4. _____ Settle down; descend; grow quiet

5. _____ A wet swampy bog

6. _____ To polish

7. _____ Not inclined to talk

8. _____ Crafty deceit

9. _____ Childish, whiny or rude

10. _____ Diffusing warmth and friendliness

Amiable	Composure	Morass	Taciturn
Artisan	Consign	Petulance	Tryst
Bourgeois	Guile	Quotidian	Virtue
Burnish	Hypothetical	Recapitulate	Wheedle
Cherish	Mitigate	Subside	Wry

Word List #2

11. _____ To influence by flattering

12. _____ To be attached to

13. _____ A secret meeting of lovers

14 _____ Commit irrevocably

15. _____ To sum up

16. _____ A middle-class person

17. _____ Daily or ordinary

18. _____ Amusing

19. _____ A craftsman

20. _____ To make less violent

Amiable	Composure	Morass	Taciturn
Artisan	Consign	Petulance	Tryst
Bourgeois	Guile	Quotidian	Virtue
Burnish	Hypothetical	Recapitulate	Wheedle
Cherish	Mitigate	Subside	Wry

Word Scramble #2

1. ACEELNPTU   P_____
2. AABEILM   A_____
3. CEHHIRS   C_____
4. AEGIIMTT   M_____
5. ACEHHILOPTTY   H_____
6. RWY   W_____
7. AAINRST   A_____
8. DEEEHLW   W_____
9. AACEEILPRTTU   R_____
10. BHINRSU   B_____
11. CEMOOPRSU   C_____
12. RSTTY   T_____
13. CGINNOS   C_____
14. BEGIOORSU   B_____
15. BDEISSU   S_____
16. ADIINOQTU   Q_____
17. AMORSS   M_____
18. EIRTUV   V_____
19. EGILU   G_____
20. ACINRTTU   T_____

Word Search #2

```
E F D O D Q A M I A B L E Z
V T M G K Q R R F Z G Y F K
M L M W R O T Y J I F U W R
A Q C H E R I S H D B N P W
N U O E C K S F Y G K R E Z
N O N E A M A O P X U N T W
L T S D P D N T O S B I U F
J I I L I S C A T L O T L S
O D G E T P O C H W U T A E
I I N U U A M I E B R X N V
F A H P L M P T T U G Y C E
J N L V A I O U I R E T E V
S N Y Z T T S R C N O D Z A
W L U R E I U N A I I D L R
L P U D Y G R V L S S T L B
W Y Q R I A E Q B H S Y S C
R X M O Z T Y U U Y S P O W
X A J T K E S O R W Z K F N
Z H T V V I R T U E P H I Q
K Y S S Z F Y C L R Z L J G
```

Crossword Clues #2

Across

4. To be attached to
6. Childish, whiny or rude
7. Daily or ordinary
8. To polish
11. To make less violent
13. Amusing
14. Calmness
16. Crafty deceit
17. A secret meeting of lovers
18. Diffusing warmth and friendliness

Down

1. Not inclined to talk
2. To sum up
3. Commit irrevocably
5. A craftsman
8. A middle-class person
9. Supposed or assumed true
10. A wet swampy bog
12. A particular moral excellence
13. To influence by flattering
15. Settle down; descend; grow quiet

Crossword Puzzle #2

Word List #3

1. _____ Capable of being accomplished

2. _____ Having a bodily form

3. _____ To be indecisive

4. _____ A pause from doing something

5. _____ Wickedness

6. _____ Most typical example of something

7. _____ Socially proper

8. _____ Brightly shining

9. _____ Sleeping

10. _____ To charm

Apathetic	Credulity	Enthrall	Luminous
Archetypal	Decorous	Expedite	Relegate
Assuage	Depravity	Feasible	Reservoir
Brevity	Dither	Incarnate	Respite
Collateral	Dormant	Indefatigable	Salve

Word List #3

11. _____ Incapable of defeat

12. _____ To assign to the proper place

13. _____ A large supply of something

14 _____ To ease

15. _____ A soothing balm

16. _____ Readiness to believe

17. _____ Lacking concern

18. _____ To speed up

19. _____ Shortness or conciseness

20. _____ Accompanying; concomitant

Apathetic	Credulity	Enthrall	Luminous
Archetypal	Decorous	Expedite	Relegate
Assuage	Depravity	Feasible	Reservoir
Brevity	Dither	Incarnate	Respite
Collateral	Dormant	Indefatigable	Salve

Word Scramble #3

1. EEIORRRSV   R _____
2. AEHLLNRT   E _____
3. BEIRTVY   B _____
4. AACEHIPTT   A _____
5. ADEIPRTVY   D _____
6. ADMNORT   D _____
7. ILMNOSUU   L _____
8. ABEEFILS   F _____
9. EEIPRST   R _____
10. DEEEIPTX   E _____
11. AACEINNRT   I _____
12. DEHIRT   D _____
13. AACEHLPRTY   A _____
14. AACELLLORT   C _____
15. AELSV   S _____
16. CDEOORSU   D _____
17. AAEGSSU   A _____
18. AEEEGLRT   R _____
19. CDEILRTUY   C _____
20. AABDEEFGIILNT   I _____

Word Search #3

```
U Y B G K J O Z R Z P D R E
Q E R R V B J A X P F F V I
J H E L B P N E J I E L N N
A A T S R H J C F R A U X D
I B E S R B F A L S S M B E
A R C H E T Y P A L I I X F
I E C V X D R E D R B N Y A
B V R L K U I E D E L O S T
E I E C R Y C K L S E U C I
R T D O R M A N T E O S V G
K Y U L D O M Y T R G Z E A
S A L L K E O I O V E A N B
I P I A A E P C X O X H T L
Q A T T R S E R E I P V H E
P T Y E E D S M A R E E R L
A H T R G D I U A V D A A O
Z E C A C Q J T A K I B L Y
H T K L E E K N H G T T L N
D I N C A R N A T E E G Y W
A C N M N C N X Y F R V R H
```

23

Crossword Clues #3

Across

2. To be indecisive
6. Socially proper
7. To ease
8. Shortness or conciseness
12. Capable of being accomplished
16. To charm
17. To assign to the proper place
18. Wickedness
19. Most typical example of something

Down

1. Brightly shining
3. Incapable of defeat
4. To speed up
5. Sleeping
7. Lacking concern
9. A large supply of something
10. Readiness to believe
11. Having a bodily form
13. A soothing balm
14. Accompanying; concomitant
15. A pause from doing something

Crossword Puzzle #3

Word List #4

1. _____ To wither away

2. _____ Shrewdness

3. _____ Suitable for drinking

4. _____ Intended to rectify

5. _____ Not suitable or capable

6. _____ Arranged

7. _____ Actively changing

8. _____ Agreeable to the taste

9. _____ To support

10. _____ Find repugnant

Abhor	Atrophy	Inept	Potable
Alacrity	Buttress	Lurid	Remedial
Ambivalent	Choreographed	Palatable	Serendipity
Amorphous	Dynamic	Peripheral	Solitude
Antagonism	Impertinent	Perspicacity	Vehement

26

Word List #4

11. _____ Ghastly

12. _____ Eagerness

13. _____ Unexpected good luck

14 _____ Showing strong feeling; forceful

15. _____ Hostility

16. _____ On or near an edge

17. _____ Without definite shape

18. _____ Having opposing feelings

19. _____ Rude

20. _____ A state of social isolation

Abhor	Atrophy	Inept	Potable
Alacrity	Buttress	Lurid	Remedial
Ambivalent	Choreographed	Palatable	Serendipity
Amorphous	Dynamic	Peripheral	Solitude
Antagonism	Impertinent	Perspicacity	Vehement

Word Scramble #4

1.	AEEHILPPRR	P _____
2.	DEEIINPRSTY	S _____
3.	ADEEILMR	R _____
4.	EINPT	I _____
5.	ACDEEGHHOOPRR	C _____
6.	AAABELLPT	P _____
7.	AAGIMNNOST	A _____
8.	BERSSTTU	B _____
9.	AACILRTY	A _____
10.	ACCEIIPPRSTY	P _____
11.	ACDIMNY	D _____
12.	AHOPRTY	A _____
13.	AABEILMNTV	A _____
14.	DEILOSTU	S _____
15.	EEIIMNNPRTT	I _____
16.	RAOBH	A _____
17.	AHMOOPRSU	A _____
18.	DILRU	L _____
19.	ABELOPT	P _____
20.	EEEHMNTV	V _____

Word Search #4

```
L V T M K E R Q D L U R I D
R A A I X S S I N E P T E S
W F B S O O B W L D W H W C
N I D I I L D B Y W P S I O
K P E E V I A N C A S M D R
P Q Y R U T L X R E A I O P
B R C B A U P G R N M H L E
K Z Q L P D O T Y N B A Q R
J N A V I E T D W A I L A I
C P V L R U A J H D V A M P
C S E O B A B G E E A C O H
M X H H M Y L M E T L R R E
W C E G Z H E M W V E I P R
E L M A T R O P H Y N T H A
Z S E R E N D I P I T Y O L
O Q N E D O H G T W F L U D
U Q T B A N T A G O N I S M
L I M P E R T I N E N T X O
M R D Q J X M H W B K G Q F
W P E R S P I C A C I T Y D
```

29

Crossword Clues #4

Across

1. Shrewdness
5. A state of social isolation
6. Rude
8. Not suitable or capable
11. Agreeable to the taste or sensibilities
12. Having opposing feelings
14. Intended to rectify or improve
15. On or near an edge
17. Actively changing
19. Unexpected good luck

Down

2. Without definite shape or type
3. Showing strong feeling; forceful
4. To support
7. Hostility
9. Arranged
10. Ghastly
12. Eagerness
13. Suitable for drinking
16. To wither away
18. Find repugnant

Crossword Puzzle #4

Word List #5

1. _____ One who excels in an art

2. _____ Incapable of correction

3. _____ Make reparations for

4. _____ Trifling

5. _____ A noisy quarrel

6. _____ Stern

7. _____ To bring about

8. _____ To change or alter in form

9. _____ Impossible to subdue

10. _____ To stray from the topic

Abject	Compensate	Fracas	Inexorable
Affront	Digress	Impervious	Latent
Appease	Dour	Incorrigible	Nominal
Apprehend	Engender	Indignant	Transmute
Colossus	Flabbergasted	Indomitable	Virtuoso

Word List #5

11. _____ A gigantic statue or thing

12. _____ Astounded

13. _____ Hidden

14 _____ To calm

15. _____ An insult

16. _____ Angry

17. _____ Incapable of being persuaded

18. _____ Impenetrable

19. _____ To seize

20. _____ Wretched

Abject	Compensate	Fracas	Inexorable
Affront	Digress	Impervious	Latent
Appease	Dour	Incorrigible	Nominal
Apprehend	Engender	Indignant	Transmute
Colossus	Flabbergasted	Indomitable	Virtuoso

Word Scramble #5

1. AILMNNO — N _____
2. DEEEGNNR — E _____
3. ADGIINNNT — I _____
4. ABDEIILMNOT — I _____
5. AEMNRSTTU — T _____
6. ABEEILNORX — I _____
7. CLOOSSSU — C _____
8. ADEEHNPPR — A _____
9. AAEEPPS — A _____
10. BACEJT — A _____
11. IOORSTUV — V _____
12. AELNTT — L _____
13. DEGIRSS — D _____
14. AABBDEEFGLRST — F _____
15. AACFRS — F _____
16. AFFNORT — A _____
17. BCEGIIILNORR — I _____
18. EIIMOPRSUV — I _____
19. ACEEMNOPST — C _____
20. UORD — D _____

Word Search #5

```
I  N  C  O  R  R  I  G  I  B  L  E  M  G
C  O  L  O  S  S  U  S  I  E  X  B  T  V
C  M  H  Q  A  V  I  R  T  U  O  S  O  L
G  E  V  C  M  M  M  A  P  Z  Z  U  N  B
B  G  A  O  G  X  S  A  F  F  R  O  N  T
A  R  E  I  Q  N  F  P  R  I  H  A  W  J
F  B  A  M  E  D  L  P  R  S  F  P  A  S
J  T  J  P  G  N  A  R  A  M  C  P  S  G
G  U  M  E  W  N  B  E  L  A  T  E  N  T
I  O  I  R  C  C  B  H  R  T  R  A  H  W
C  N  N  V  V  T  E  E  F  G  P  S  E  I
R  Y  D  I  N  C  R  N  I  Y  T  E  I  L
L  I  I  O  O  U  G  D  O  U  R  W  T  Z
L  U  G  U  M  U  A  O  G  E  A  B  E  Q
X  V  N  S  I  I  S  V  D  V  N  F  E  P
S  H  A  W  N  M  T  N  Q  V  S  A  B  H
K  B  N  E  A  Q  E  A  V  X  M  Z  Z  T
C  F  T  Z  L  G  D  N  B  H  U  P  D  L
N  K  V  D  N  H  T  D  V  L  T  S  B  Y
K  I  N  E  X  O  R  A  B  L  E  D  D  L
```

Crossword Clues #5

Across

1. Incapable of being persuaded
4. Trifling
6. Impenetrable
7. Make reparations for
9. Stern
13. Impossible to subdue
14. Angry
16. Wretched
17. To stray from the topic
18. To change or alter in form
19. To seize

Down

2. To bring about
3. A noisy quarrel
5. An insult
6. Incapable of correction
8. To calm
10. One who excels in an art
11. Astounded
12. A gigantic statue or thing
15. Hidden

Crossword Puzzle #5

Word List #6

1. _____ Respect

2. _____ Rude and bad-tempered

3. _____ Offering no resistance

4. _____ Speed

5. _____ A beginner

6. _____ Excessive greed

7. _____ Obtainable

8. _____ A curse

9. _____ To emphasize something

10. _____ Acutely insightful and wise

Accentuate	Celerity	Novice	Surly
Accessible	Compliant	Paradigm	Tenable
Approbation	Deference	Plaudits	Tentative
Aspersion	Idiosyncratic	Saccharine	Upbraid
Avarice	Indigent	Sagacious	Wistful

Word List #6

11. _____ To criticize or scold severely

12. _____ Defensible

13. _____ Enthusiastic approval

14. _____ Full of yearning; musingly sad

15. _____ A standard or typical example

16. _____ Very poor

17. _____ Peculiar to the individual

18. _____ Unsettled in mind or opinion

19. _____ Overly sweet

20. _____ Praise

Accentuate	Celerity	Novice	Surly
Accessible	Compliant	Paradigm	Tenable
Approbation	Deference	Plaudits	Tentative
Aspersion	Idiosyncratic	Saccharine	Upbraid
Avarice	Indigent	Sagacious	Wistful

Word Scramble #6

1. AACCEENTTU   A _____
2. ACILMNOPT   C _____
3. CDEEEEFNR   D _____
4. LCEEIRTY   C _____
5. AACGIOSSU   S _____
6. DEGIINNT   I _____
7. ADILPSTU   P _____
8. ABCCEEILSS   A _____
9. FILSTUW   W _____
10. LRSUY   S _____
11. ABEELNT   T _____
12. AEINOPRSS   A _____
13. BAAINOOPPRT   A _____
14. AACCEHINRS   S _____
15. AEEINTTTV   T _____
16. DABIPRU   U _____
17. IACCDIINORSTY   I _____
18. RAACEIV   A _____
19. CEINOV   N _____
20. AADGIMPR   P _____

Word Search #6

```
E  I  R  N  C  O  M  P  L  I  A  N  T  L
A  C  C  E  N  T  U  A  T  E  O  M  T  X
I  U  Z  D  E  F  E  R  E  N  C  E  O  G
C  A  P  P  R  O  B  A  T  I  O  N  V  T
I  C  L  B  O  U  N  D  G  O  N  C  I  I
W  C  A  M  R  S  W  I  S  T  F  U  L  D
L  E  U  T  Q  A  P  G  O  I  N  N  T  I
U  S  D  G  J  Q  I  M  A  N  Y  N  E  O
D  S  I  E  T  L  N  D  M  D  V  B  N  S
N  I  T  D  T  E  F  R  N  I  C  Q  A  Y
U  B  S  P  F  O  N  C  T  G  E  I  B  N
E  L  R  A  J  Z  T  T  O  E  L  A  L  C
M  E  Z  X  G  T  O  T  A  N  E  K  E  R
I  Q  U  J  Q  A  R  E  Y  T  R  C  P  A
X  K  S  S  A  C  C  H  A  R  I  N  E  T
X  A  W  U  Z  I  R  I  E  V  T  V  B  I
Y  F  E  Y  R  N  B  N  O  T  Y  G  E  C
B  B  E  A  V  L  L  N  D  U  T  G  M  Y
K  E  V  M  C  J  Y  O  U  Y  S  C  T  S
A  A  S  P  E  R  S  I  O  N  V  U  V  V
```

Crossword Clues #6

Across

1. Praise
3. Excessive greed
7. Full of yearning; musingly sad
8. A curse
10. To emphasize something
11. A standard or typical example
16. Offering no resistance
17. Obtainable
19. Respect
20. Enthusiastic approval

Down

2. Peculiar to the individual
4. Speed
5. Rude and bad-tempered
6. Overly sweet
9. Acutely insightful and wise
12. Unsettled in mind or opinion
13. A beginner
14. Very poor
15. To criticize or scold severely
18. Defensible

Crossword Puzzle #6

Word List #7

1. _____ Obtaining another's property by theft

2. _____ Sedate

3. _____ An absence of emotion or enthusiasm

4. _____ To swell out

5. _____ Having a pointed

6. _____ To introduce a microorganism

7. _____ Hungry to an extreme degree

8. _____ A feeling of ill will

9. _____ Unformed or formless

10 _____ Obvious to the eye or mind

Accede	Distend	Iridescent	Semaphore
Animosity	Expedient	Larceny	Staid
Apathy	Impinge	Pungent	Tangential
Conspicuous	Inchoate	Ravenous	Vex
Contemporaneous	Inoculate	Resolution	Vilify

Word List #7

11. _____ A decision to do something

12. _____ Advisable

13. _____ To confuse or annoy

14 _____ Showing rainbow colors

15. _____ To agree

16. _____ To impact

17. _____ To lower in importance

18. _____ Incidental

19. _____ Existing during the same time

20. _____ A visual signal

Accede	Distend	Iridescent	Semaphore
Animosity	Expedient	Larceny	Staid
Apathy	Impinge	Pungent	Tangential
Conspicuous	Inchoate	Ravenous	Vex
Contemporaneous	Inoculate	Resolution	Vilify

Word Scramble #7

1. DDEINST   D _____
2. EGIIMNP   I _____
3. ACEEMNNOOOPRSTU   C _____
4. CDEEIINRST   I _____
5. CACDEE   A _____
6. FIILVY   V _____
7. ACEHINOT   I _____
8. ANAEGILNTT   T _____
9. DEEEINPTX   E _____
10. EILNOORSTU   R _____
11. AAHPTY   A _____
12. AEEHMOPRS   S _____
13. EVX   V _____
14. CCINOOPSSUU   C _____
15. EGNNPTU   P _____
16. ADIST   S _____
17. ACELNRY   L _____
18. ACEILNOTU   I _____
19. AENORSUV   R _____
20. MAIINOSTY   A _____

Word Search #7

```
B Z R O I E C V V J H S Z I
P O M B A N I M O S I T Y Y
C L V L U R T J P G R C Z S
T Y I A P A T H Y Q I O O M
X Y L Y C V S T A I D N B Y
F T I N O C U L A T E T P A
I A F H P Z E I V D S E Q G
N N Y F P E X D A V C M Z P
R G V V C S P P E I E P C L
W E R S P N E G X D N O F I
W N S A U J D M L U T R Q N
Y T E O V V I O A C R A C C
I I X S L E E Y C P W N L H
D A K M A U N X K Z H E F O
D L C Q R F T O P K J O K A
A S K R C K F I U Z X U R T
D I S T E N D R O S O S N E
I M P I N G E P U N G E N T
Q A D Z Y Z R L J M A V K J
C O N S P I C U O U S J G Q
```

47

Crossword Clues #7

Across

1. To swell out
6. Obtaining another's property by theft
7. Obvious to the eye or mind
10. Sedate
12. Incidental
15. To impact
16. Unformed or formless
17. Having a pointed
18. To lower in importance
19. To introduce a microorganism

Down

2. Showing rainbow colors
3. Hungry to an extreme degree
4. Advisable
5. A decision to do something
8. A visual signal
9. Existing during the same time
11. An absence of emotion or enthusiasm
13. To agree
14. A feeling of ill will
18. To confuse or annoy

Crossword Puzzle #7

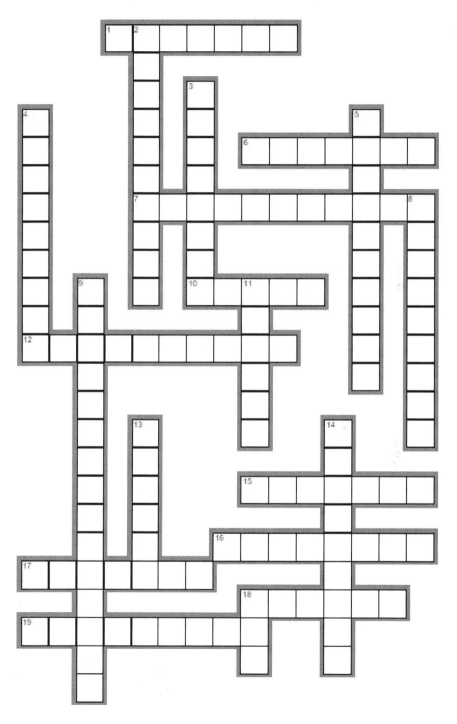

Word List #8

1. _____ Able to be heard

2. _____ Excessive

3. _____ To disappear

4. _____ Not secure

5. _____ Wealth or success

6. _____ Lacking quickness of intellect

7. _____ Praise, glorify, or honor

8. _____ To evaluate

9. _____ Taken directly from a source

10. _____ Disposed or willing to comply

Acerbic	Artifact	Contentious	Laud
Adorn	Assess	Derivative	Obtuse
Amenable	Audible	Dissipate	Pariah
Antipathy	Cerebral	Exorbitant	Precarious
Arbitration	Commendation	Indolence	Prosperity

Word List #8

11. _____ To decorate

12. _____ Sour in taste or harsh in tone

13. _____ Having a tendency to quarrel

14. _____ A strong dislike

15. _____ A notice of recognition

16. _____ An outcast

17. _____ Related to the intellect

18. _____ Man-made with cultural significance

19. _____ Inactivity from a dislike of work

20. _____ The act of resolving a dispute

Acerbic	Artifact	Contentious	Laud
Adorn	Assess	Derivative	Obtuse
Amenable	Audible	Dissipate	Pariah
Antipathy	Cerebral	Exorbitant	Precarious
Arbitration	Commendation	Indolence	Prosperity

Word Scramble #8

1. ACDEIMMNNOOT   C _____
2. NRADO   A _____
3. SSAESS   A _____
4. CEINNOOSTTU   C _____
5. BEOSTU   O _____
6. ABCEELRR   C _____
7. ABCCEIR   A _____
8. AABIINORRTT   A _____
9. CDEEILNNO   I _____
10. AACFIRTT   A _____
11. EIOPPRRSTY   P _____
12. ACEIOPRRSU   P _____
13. ADEIIPSST   D _____
14. ADLU   L _____
15. AAHINPTTY   A _____
16. ABDEILU   A _____
17. ADEEIIRTVV   D _____
18. AABEELMN   A _____
19. AAHIPR   P _____
20. ABEINORTTX   E _____

Word Search #8

```
K P L R D E R I V A T I V E
W Y A C E R B I C D A E D O
B I A O L G R L K D N Z P D
X V U N F Z O V N Z T J R V
W W D T C K P R K I I K E X
F A I E V A L O D J P H C M
E A B N D K R B W X A Y A Z
V P L T D I K T L C T A R K
D L E I A O S U I I H U I H
R E A O G M L S R F Y A O R
Z C A U C T E E I C A X U X
A E U S D V P N N P E C S N
B R U J K S R A A C A S T Y
D E O A O O H Z F B E T J M
C B F R D N T Z D S L H E U
F R P A R I A H S A I E C V
B A R B I T R A T I O N Y O
P L P Y E X O R B I T A N T
N J J L X R F C L R S A W J
P V C O M M E N D A T I O N
```

Crossword Clues #8

Across

2. The act of resolving a dispute
6. Sour in taste or harsh in tone
8. Wealth or success
9. Disposed or willing to comply
12. Taken directly from a source
13. To decorate
15. Having a tendency to quarrel
16. Not secure
18. A strong dislike
19. Able to be heard

Down

1. To disappear
3. Inactivity from a dislike of work
4. A notice of recognition
5. An outcast
7. Related to the intellect
10. To evaluate
11. Praise, glorify, or honor
13. Man-made with cultural significance
14. Excessive
17. Lacking quickness of intellect

Crossword Puzzle #8

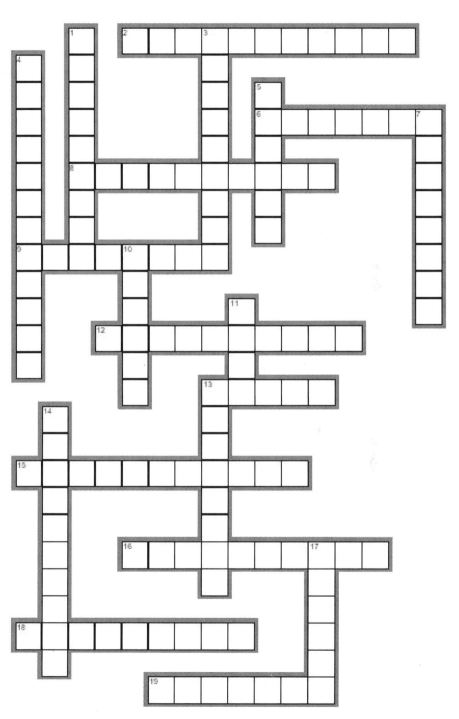

Word List #9

1. _____ Dried up

2. _____ Physical beauty

3. _____ The highest point

4. _____ Someone who is inexperienced

5. _____ Extreme vigor

6. _____ To vomit

7. _____ Separated and narrow-minded

8. _____ Defeat

9. _____ Move in a sinuous spiral

10. _____ Using, buying or eating something

Abjure	Consumption	Insular	Parched
Arbiter	Debase	Meander	Pulchritude
Ardor	Endorse	Melancholy	Regurgitate
Bequeath	Foil	Neophyte	Substantiate
Captivate	Inferred	Overcome	Zenith

Word List #9

11. _____ Conclude by reasoning; in logic

12. _____ Formally reject or disavow

13. _____ To thwart

14. _____ To get the attention of

15. _____ To lower the quality of something

16. _____ To verify

17. _____ Gloomy

18. _____ To pass on

19. _____ One who can resolve a dispute

20. _____ Approve of

Abjure	Consumption	Insular	Parched
Arbiter	Debase	Meander	Pulchritude
Ardor	Endorse	Melancholy	Regurgitate
Bequeath	Foil	Neophyte	Substantiate
Captivate	Inferred	Overcome	Zenith

Word Scramble #9

1. AABEINSSTTTU   S _____
2. ABEIRRT   A _____
3. EEHNOPTY   N _____
4. ABDEES   D _____
5. AACEIPTTV   C _____
6. DEEFINRR   I _____
7. ADEEMNR   M _____
8. OADRR   A _____
9. AILNRSU   I _____
10. ACDEHPR   P _____
11. FILO   F _____
12. ABEEHQTU   B _____
13. ABEJRU   A _____
14. DEENORS   E _____
15. AEEGGIRRTTU   R _____
16. CIMNNOOPSTU   C _____
17. ACEHLLMNOY   M _____
18. EHINTZ   Z _____
19. CDEHILPRTUU   P _____
20. CEEMOORV   O _____

Word Search #9

```
R Z N T G G P P A R C H E D
H R E G U R G I T A T E A A
C F O Y V K I J G A O P W V
E S P V J K X N E L S U Y B
X U H F E H N U F D B L B I
O B Y B B R Q G E E V C B M
W S T C E E C O J B R H Y E
Y T E J B J O O N A K R M A
J A K C H B N E M S H I E N
O N H N J U S T O E E T L D
X T M W H R U E H R E U A E
A I Z D O M M I T T X D N R
I A E D A P O A W T E C D
S T N Q F H T V A T S R H W
H E I R C F I J P K A M O L
B B T E A T O F T L B I L H
Q Y H I P R N I U K J F Y H
J V X A Z L D S L L U G H P
H K C P U S N O L K R Z D N
V P A R B I T E R B E N R O
```

59

Crossword Clues #9

Across

5. Approve of
7. Formally reject or disavow
9. One who can resolve a dispute
10. To get the attention of
15. To lower the quality of something
17. Dried up
18. To pass on
19. The highest point
20. To thwart

Down

1. Conclude by reasoning; in logic
2. Extreme vigor
3. To vomit
4. To verify
6. Physical beauty
8. Defeat
11. Separated and narrow-minded
12. Gloomy
13. Someone who is inexperienced
14. Move in a sinuous spiral
16. Using, buying or eating something

Crossword Puzzle #9

Word List #10

1. _____ Consisting of a diverse mix of elements

2. _____ Superiority in importance or quantity

3. _____ Not growing or changing

4. _____ To sketch out in a vague way

5. _____ To relieve

6. _____ Not obvious

7. _____ Truthfulness

8. _____ Very important and holy

9. _____ Lewd

10 _____ Secret

Adumbrate	Bolster	Incongruous	Redoubtable
Alleviate	Clandestine	Lavish	Sacrosanct
Ambiguous	Complicit	Preponderance	Stagnant
Analogous	Eclectic	Profane	Subtle
Arrogate	Fatuous	Provincial	Veracity

Word List #10

11. _____ Inspiring fear

12. _____ Being an accomplice in a wrongful act

13. _____ To take without justification

14. _____ Inconsistent or incompatible

15. _____ To offer support or strengthen

16. _____ Someone less sophisticated

17. _____ Of doubtful or uncertain nature

18. _____ Similar to

19. _____ Given without limits

20. _____ Silly

Adumbrate	Bolster	Incongruous	Redoubtable
Alleviate	Clandestine	Lavish	Sacrosanct
Ambiguous	Complicit	Preponderance	Stagnant
Analogous	Eclectic	Profane	Subtle
Arrogate	Fatuous	Provincial	Veracity

Word Scramble #10

1. AEFNOPR   P _____
2. UABGIMOSU   A _____
3. ACDEEILNNST   C _____
4. BELSTU   S _____
5. RAABDEMTU   A _____
6. AACCNORSST   S _____
7. ACIILNOPRV   P _____
8. ABBDEELORTU   R _____
9. AFOSTUU   F _____
10. CGINNOORSUU   I _____
11. CCCEEILT   E _____
12. ACEIRTVY   V _____
13. AHILSV   L _____
14. CCIILMOPT   C _____
15. BELORST   B _____
16. RAAEGORT   A _____
17. TAAGNNST   S _____
18. ACDEEENNOPPRR   P _____
19. NAAGLOOSU   A _____
20. LAAEEILTV   A _____

Word Search #10

```
S  Q  S  P  P  M  W  G  O  S  A  T  W  T
S  A  C  R  O  S  A  N  C  T  L  R  B  K
I  N  Y  E  I  B  J  L  A  A  L  E  D  S
Y  P  W  P  C  B  N  S  M  G  E  D  I  H
A  R  D  O  Q  O  B  U  B  N  V  O  F  K
W  O  Q  N  Y  L  V  B  I  A  I  U  A  U
J  V  T  D  J  S  F  T  G  N  A  B  E  G
M  I  J  E  E  T  S  L  U  T  T  T  V  I
P  N  D  R  N  E  G  E  O  Z  E  A  Z  N
S  C  V  A  D  R  N  Y  U  O  Y  B  A  C
N  I  P  N  L  A  V  I  S  H  F  L  N  O
R  A  A  C  W  A  F  M  X  A  N  E  A  N
A  L  P  E  B  J  J  A  C  T  T  S  L  G
C  O  M  P  L  I  C  I  T  A  P  V  O  R
A  R  R  O  G  A  T  E  R  U  R  A  G  U
Y  C  F  O  N  C  O  B  Y  K  O  W  O  O
X  C  I  B  E  G  M  K  F  U  F  U  U  U
Z  M  K  L  M  U  X  H  U  C  A  C  S  S
Y  E  C  Q  D  Q  Z  D  R  X  N  P  W  I
V  E  R  A  C  I  T  Y  A  S  E  D  X  P
```

Crossword Clues #10

Across

1. Consisting of a diverse mix of elements
4. Inspiring fear
6. To relieve
7. Lewd
9. Given without limits
12. Similar to
14. Inconsistent or incompatible
17. Superiority in importance or quantity
18. To sketch out in a vague way
19. Silly

Down

2. Secret
3. To offer support or strengthen
5. Very important and holy
7. Someone less sophisticated
8. To take without justification
10. Of doubtful or uncertain nature
11. Truthfulness
13. Not obvious
15. Being an accomplice in a wrongful act
16. Not growing or changing

Crossword Puzzle #10

Word List #11

1. _____ To party

2. _____ To obliterate

3. _____ To imagine or come up with

4. _____ Green in tint or color

5. _____ Longing for familiar things or persons

6. _____ Deceit used to achieve one's goal

7. _____ The condition of being unequal

8. _____ Necessary for completeness

9. _____ Lofty

10. _____ Extremely

Blithe	Disheartened	Grandiloquence	Reprehensible
Carouse	Disparity	Integral	Rife
Conceive	Domineering	Nostalgic	Subterfuge
Consolation	Expunge	Penchant	Susceptible
Convivial	Flaccid	Prohibitively	Verdant

Word List #11

11. _____ Deserving rebuke

12. _____ Feeling a loss of spirit or morale

13. _____ Arrogant and bossy

14. _____ Easily influenced or affected

15. _____ An act of comforting

16. _____ Limp

17. _____ Abundant

18. _____ A tendency

19. _____ Characterized by feasting

20. _____ Carefree, happy and lighthearted

Blithe	Disheartened	Grandiloquence	Reprehensible
Carouse	Disparity	Integral	Rife
Conceive	Domineering	Nostalgic	Subterfuge
Consolation	Expunge	Penchant	Susceptible
Convivial	Flaccid	Prohibitively	Verdant

Word Scramble #11

1. EFIR   R _____
2. BEEFGRSTUU   S _____
3. ACIILNOVV   C _____
4. CCEEINOV   C _____
5. BCEEILPSSTU   S _____
6. ADDEEEHINRST   D _____
7. ACGILNOST   N _____
8. ADENRTV   V _____
9. ADIIPRSTY   D _____
10. AEGILNRT   I _____
11. BEHILT   B _____
12. BEEEEHILNPRRS   R _____
13. BEHIIILOPRTVY   P _____
14. ACEHNNPT   P _____
15. DEEGIIMNNOR   D _____
16. EEGNPUX   E _____
17. ACEORSU   C _____
18. ACDEEGILNNNOQRU   G _____
19. ACILNNOOOST   C _____
20. ACCDFIL   F _____

Word Search #11

```
U  P  E  N  C  H  A  N  T  K  E  O  N  L
V  D  L  Y  L  C  I  N  T  E  G  R  A  L
G  I  I  D  W  Z  C  O  N  C  E  I  V  E
Y  R  O  S  O  C  V  Y  N  F  V  V  G  K
M  U  A  U  H  M  A  G  I  I  Q  U  C  S
N  Z  R  N  I  E  I  R  V  X  F  G  D  I
Q  T  H  T  D  N  A  N  O  R  E  O  Y  Y
R  K  W  N  Z  I  O  R  E  U  P  L  S  E
Z  I  B  O  A  C  L  T  T  E  S  A  P  X
Y  Y  K  S  C  S  B  O  X  E  R  E  Z  P
U  U  K  T  Q  U  W  P  Q  X  N  I  B  U
R  U  I  A  S  S  G  X  V  U  W  E  N  N
O  F  F  L  A  C  C  I  D  G  E  S  D  G
Y  O  Y  G  V  E  R  D  A  N  T  N  J  E
O  F  D  I  S  P  A  R  I  T  Y  D  C  I
A  V  I  C  I  T  K  G  B  L  I  T  H  E
O  P  R  O  H  I  B  I  T  I  V  E  L  Y
D  E  G  U  A  B  K  R  J  B  F  A  U  C
C  O  N  S  O  L  A  T  I  O  N  E  T  J
T  R  E  P  R  E  H  E  N  S  I  B  L  E
```

Crossword Clues #11

Across

4. Green in tint or color
5. Limp
6. Characterized by feasting
8. Deceit used to achieve one's goal
11. Necessary for completeness
13. Longing for familiar things or persons
15. Feeling a loss of spirit or morale
17. Deserving rebuke
18. Carefree, happy and lighthearted
19. To obliterate
20. Lofty

Down

1. Extremely
2. A tendency
3. An act of comforting
7. Easily influenced or affected
9. The condition of being unequal
10. To party
12. Arrogant and bossy
14. To imagine or come up with
16. Abundant

Crossword Puzzle #11

Word List #12

1. _____ Short-lived or temporary

2. _____ To voice disapproval

3. _____ Easily angered

4. _____ An agreement

5. _____ Charitable giving to help others

6. _____ Charming

7. _____ An atmosphere of good cheer

8. _____ Lenient, or overly generous

9. _____ To fluctuate

10. _____ Well-spoken

Accord	Bonhomie	Extricate	Philanthropy
Aggrieve	Chide	Indulgent	Pretentious
Allege	Cordial	Ineffable	Transitory
Articulate	Despondent	Irascible	Vacillate
Benefactor	Effrontery	Perfunctory	Winsome

Word List #12

11. _____ Cause to feel distress

12. _____ Supporter who gives aid

13. _____ Done with minimal effort

14. _____ Warm

15. _____ Tawdry or vulgar

16. _____ To disentangle

17. _____ Impudence

18. _____ Unspeakable

19. _____ Feeling depressed

20. _____ To assert

Accord	Bonhomie	Extricate	Philanthropy
Aggrieve	Chide	Indulgent	Pretentious
Allege	Cordial	Ineffable	Transitory
Articulate	Despondent	Irascible	Vacillate
Benefactor	Effrontery	Perfunctory	Winsome

Word Scramble #12

1. ACCDOR   A _____
2. EEINOPRSTTU   P _____
3. BEHIMNOO   B _____
4. CDEHI   C _____
5. ABCEEFNORT   B _____
6. AHHILNOPPRTY   P _____
7. AEEGLL   A _____
8. ACEEIRTTX   E _____
9. EIMNOSW   W _____
10. DDEENNOPST   D _____
11. ABEEFFILN   I _____
12. AACEILRTTU   A _____
13. DEGILNNTU   I _____
14. AEEGGIRV   A _____
15. AINORRSTTY   T _____
16. AACEILLTV   V _____
17. CEFNOPRRTUY   P _____
18. EEFFNORRTY   E _____
19. ACDILOR   C _____
20. ABCEIILRS   I _____

Word Search #12

```
G D H T R I N D U L G E N T
E H E H A N R W D Z M V C Z
O Q J N E O E B D O H B J E
T I H H C A T E S E G J P O
V R K C A E I N N F P T H I
I D A V F M I E I F Z J I R
Z E N N O W D F L R T I L W
B S Y H S I E A M O P R A P
U P N D H I I C E N E A N V
Z O S C N D T T C T R S T X
B N P H R G A O O E F C H A
O D M O V C G R R R U I R R
Y E C L I W G V L Y N B O T
W N A R F Y R Q I N C L P I
Z T T V A C I L L A T E Y C
J X P R E T E N T I O U S U
E I P R X L V J K T R U P L
V T I A L L E G E S Y S C A
C K A Y Y P C I A S U X X T
I J Z C N I N E F F A B L E
```

Crossword Clues #12

Across

2. Tawdry or vulgar
4. Well-spoken
6. Supporter who gives aid
8. Cause to feel distress
11. To voice disapproval
13. Charitable giving to help others
14. Lenient, or overly generous
19. Charming
20. Short-lived or temporary

Down

1. Easily angered
3. Unspeakable
5. To disentangle
7. Impudence
9. To fluctuate
10. Warm
12. Done with minimal effort
15. Feeling depressed
16. To assert
17. An agreement
18. An atmosphere of good cheer

Crossword Puzzle #12

Word List #13

1. _____ Impossible to pacify

2. _____ Ready to fight

3. _____ Giving off intense heat

4. _____ A selected collection of writings

5. _____ Negligent

6. _____ Small in quantity

7. _____ Conventional

8. _____ Being of crucial importance

9. _____ Of good reputation

10. _____ Harsh

Anthology	Hallowed	Orthodox	Reputable
Aversion	Implacable	Panacea	Submissive
Callous	Indolent	Paucity	Torrid
Contemporary	Ingenuous	Pivotal	Truculent
Ebullient	Notorious	Remiss	Uniform

Word List #13

11. _____ Belonging to the present

12. _____ Slothful

13. _____ Extremely lively

14. _____ A particular dislike for something

15. _____ Easily yielding to authority

16. _____ Widely and unfavorably known

17. _____ Always the same

18. _____ Open and sincere

19. _____ A remedy for all ills or difficulties

20. _____ Revered

Anthology	Hallowed	Orthodox	Reputable
Aversion	Implacable	Panacea	Submissive
Callous	Indolent	Paucity	Torrid
Contemporary	Ingenuous	Pivotal	Truculent
Ebullient	Notorious	Remiss	Uniform

Word Scramble #13

1. AGHLNOOTY   A _____
2. ACIPTUY   P _____
3. AAACENP   P _____
4. EGINNOSUU   I _____
5. ACLLOSU   C _____
6. AABCEILLMP   I _____
7. ACEMNOOPRRTY   C _____
8. EIMRSS   R _____
9. BEIIMSSSUV   S _____
10. CELNRTTUU   T _____
11. ABEELPRTU   R _____
12. DEILNNOT   I _____
13. DHOOORTX   O _____
14. AILOPTV   P _____
15. DIORRT   T _____
16. FIMNORU   U _____
17. BEEILLNTU   E _____
18. ADEHLLOW   H _____
19. INOOORSTU   N _____
20. AEINORSV   A _____

Word Search #13

```
M C D N B W J S K U U X T B
C B W C Z F R A F V O I P E
E B U L L I E N T D B J C S
J X X U J C P T O E F P B U
Y Q V E A S U H B D T N E B
M O H N L P T O K S R D F M
T J A D M R A L Z L U S T I
A P L U O E B O M Z C K P S
W M L Z X M L G C L U E I S
A B O M T I E Y O T L F N I
B V W Z P S U Q N A E T G V
N E E R E S L E T V N L E E
O Z D R F C L O E K T S N H
P C Q O S O V U M W S Y U Q
M A H Z D I E R P G Q X O L
Z L U N P N O T O R I O U S
W L I C X F D N R G H H S I
F O E A I M P L A C A B L E
B U L N X T T O R R I D F B
R S U T L P Y M Y F S C R D
```

83

Crossword Clues #13

Across

2. Impossible to pacify
5. Being of crucial importance
6. Belonging to the present
7. Giving off intense heat
13. A selected collection of writings
15. Ready to fight
17. Widely and unfavorably known
18. Always the same
19. Negligent

Down

1. Revered
2. Open and sincere
3. Small in quantity
4. A particular dislike for something
8. Of good reputation
9. Harsh
10. Slothful
11. Extremely lively
12. Conventional
14. Easily yielding to authority
16. A remedy for all ills or difficulties

Crossword Puzzle #13

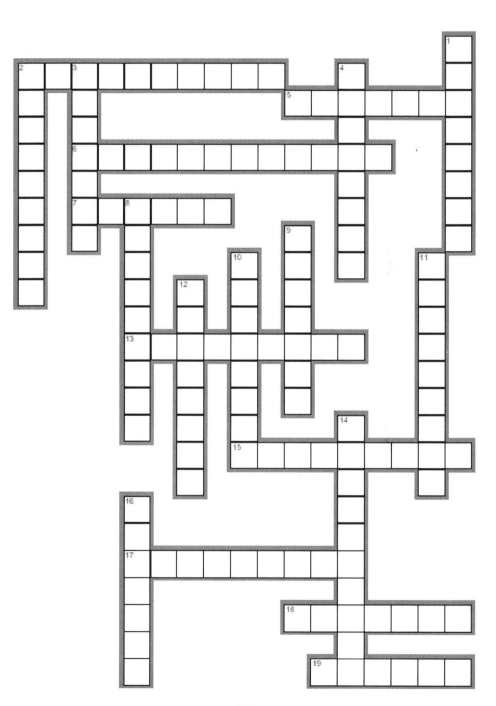

Word List #14

1. _____ Winding

2. _____ Sickeningly sweet

3. _____ Express passionately

4. _____ Graceful

5. _____ Relating to memory

6. _____ To assist the development of

7. _____ A burden

8. _____ Customs and conventions

9. _____ Loss of sensation

10. _____ Sedateness

Amass	Emollient	Mores	Rhapsodize
Anesthesia	Inclined	Multifarious	Sobriety
Bane	Lithe	Negligent	Temperance
Cloying	Litigant	Nurture	Tortuous
Deliberate	Mnemonic	Plenitude	Utopia

Word List #14

11. _____ Having great diversity or variety

12. _____ Moderation in action or thought

13. _____ Bring together or assemble

14. _____ Ideal and perfect place

15. _____ Intentional

16. _____ Habitually careless

17. _____ Soothing

18. _____ Tending towards something

19. _____ An abundance

20. _____ Someone engaged in a lawsuit

Amass	Emollient	Mores	Rhapsodize
Anesthesia	Inclined	Multifarious	Sobriety
Bane	Lithe	Negligent	Temperance
Cloying	Litigant	Nurture	Tortuous
Deliberate	Mnemonic	Plenitude	Utopia

Word Scramble #14

1. ADEHIOPRSZ   R _____
2. ACEEEMNPRT   T _____
3. CGILNOY   C _____
4. AAMSS   A _____
5. AIOPTU   U _____
6. ABDEEEILRT   D _____
7. CEIMMNNO   M _____
8. AFIILMORSTUU   M _____
9. BEIORSTY   S _____
10. AAEEHINSST   A _____
11. DEEILNPTU   P _____
12. EEGGILNNT   N _____
13. CDEIILNN   I _____
14. ENRRTUU   N _____
15. EMORS   M _____
16. OORSTTUU   T _____
17. ABEN   B _____
18. EHILT   L _____
19. AGIILNTT   L _____
20. EEILLMNOT   E _____

Word Search #14

```
R  H  A  P  S  O  D  I  Z  E  Y  K  S  F
C  D  L  A  V  A  M  A  S  S  Z  U  U  J
I  Q  S  S  I  P  C  B  I  L  O  A  Z  U
E  F  M  L  L  G  N  M  L  U  S  N  C  T
P  Q  Z  P  N  P  D  A  T  V  L  E  L  E
T  M  J  T  E  H  Q  R  Q  F  A  S  O  M
D  U  D  P  G  S  O  B  R  I  E  T  Y  P
B  L  Z  Z  L  T  Q  B  X  Q  Z  H  I  E
U  T  O  P  I  A  O  P  L  I  Y  E  N  R
Q  I  B  B  G  N  T  S  Z  Y  D  S  G  A
A  F  M  Z  E  G  C  K  L  X  E  I  W  N
B  A  N  E  N  U  G  L  F  J  L  A  I  C
V  R  Q  P  T  R  J  C  I  L  I  T  H  E
O  I  S  M  B  G  I  V  H  N  B  B  N  U
Q  O  P  L  E  N  I  T  U  D  E  P  U  P
M  U  I  E  O  E  O  O  Z  T  R  D  R  F
P  S  Z  M  U  L  I  T  I  G  A  N  T  E
I  K  E  M  O  L  L  I  E  N  T  B  U  A
C  N  A  L  K  J  D  H  M  Z  E  G  R  E
M  O  R  E  S  Z  J  Q  H  G  F  U  E  W
```

Crossword Clues #14

Across

2. Moderation in action or thought
3. Express passionately
5. Sedateness
8. An abundance
9. Sickeningly sweet
11. Someone engaged in a lawsuit
15. Winding
16. Having great diversity or variety
17. Soothing
20. Loss of sensation

Down

1. Intentional
4. Habitually careless
6. A burden
7. Ideal and perfect place
10. Bring together or assemble
12. To assist the development of
13. Relating to memory
14. Tending towards something
18. Customs and conventions
19. Graceful

Crossword Puzzle #14

Word List #15

1. _____ A large book

2. _____ Based on observation

3. _____ Very clever

4. _____ Not changeable

5. _____ Happening by chance

6. _____ Firm

7. _____ A detested person or thing

8. _____ Brotherhood

9. _____ To grant the vote to

10. _____ An agreement of opinion

Anathema	Consensus	Empirical	Platitude
Astute	Covet	Enfranchise	Resolute
Camaraderie	Disclose	Fortuitous	Sapient
Censor	Divulge	Immutable	Tome
Congeal	Elegy	Inveterate	Valid

Word List #15

11. _____ Acutely insightful and wise

12. _____ To desire enviously

13. _____ To thicken into a solid

14. _____ Suppress objectionable content

15. _____ Poem of lamentation

16. _____ Well grounded in logic or truth

17. _____ An uninspired remark

18. _____ To reveal

19. _____ To reveal something secret

20. _____ Stubbornly established by habit

Anathema	Consensus	Empirical	Platitude
Astute	Covet	Enfranchise	Resolute
Camaraderie	Disclose	Fortuitous	Sapient
Censor	Divulge	Immutable	Tome
Congeal	Elegy	Inveterate	Valid

Word Scramble #15

1. ABEILMMTU   I _____
2. EMOT   T _____
3. AEINPST   S _____
4. EELORSTU   R _____
5. AAACDEEIMRR   C _____
6. FIOORSTTUU   F _____
7. DEGILUV   D _____
8. EEGLY   E _____
9. ADEILPTTU   P _____
10. ACEIILMPR   E _____
11. RCENOS   C _____
12. AESTTU   A _____
13. CDEILOSS   D _____
14. ACEGLNO   C _____
15. ACEEFHINNRS   E _____
16. CEOTV   C _____
17. CENNOSSSU   C _____
18. AEEEINRTTV   I _____
19. ADILV   V _____
20. AAAEHMNT   A _____

Word Search #15

```
C O N S E N S U S O U E O X
B Q D C R E S O L U T E A K
T M I A Z R V L A R G N D T
G E S M L Q D M J L X F J P
T M C A B A A R U H I R U Q
K P L R T W K V P B N A A L
O I O A H A I P L Z V N L M
J R S D P D M T A R E C J Y
Q I E E T O M E T D T H S F
A C R R A G U J I T E I L I
S A P I E N T L T K R S A U
Q L X E H I A F U L A E F C
P E I I J V B D D G T S K O
H Z Y W A R L O E U E V T N
A T C U W C E S T E F Z R G
W L I K M O E S X T L A N E
W S H X Z V A N A T H E M A
R J E I L E E U S Y I L G L
P E F O R T U I T O U S R Y
C V I Q D K M K G C R X N A
```

Crossword Clues #15

Across

1. To grant the vote to
4. An agreement of opinion
5. Well grounded in logic or truth
7. Firm
8. An uninspired remark
10. To reveal something secret
11. A large book
12. To desire enviously
13. Acutely insightful and wise
15. Very clever
19. Brotherhood

Down

2. To thicken into a solid
3. Happening by chance
6. Stubbornly established by habit
9. Not changeable
14. Poem of lamentation
15. A detested person or thing
16. To reveal
17. Based on observation
18. Suppress objectionable content

Crossword Puzzle #15

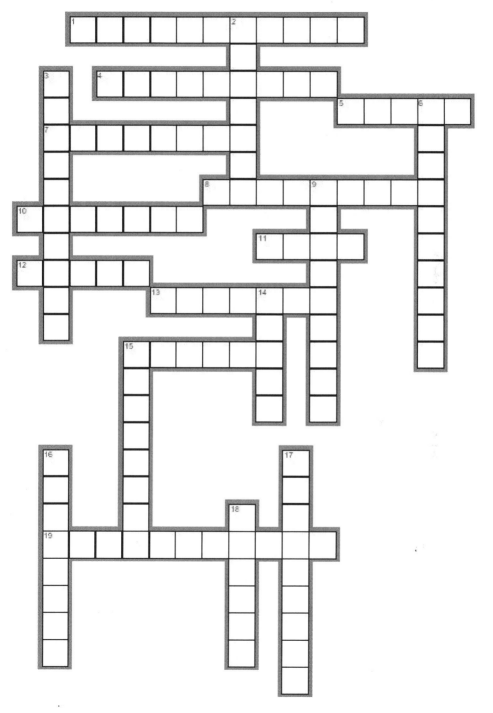

Word List #16

1. _____ Spreading widely throughout

2. _____ To prevent

3. _____ Suitable for growing crops

4. _____ Members of christian holy orders

5. _____ Boring and unoriginal

6. _____ To insert between other things

7. _____ Secret agreement

8. _____ A source of danger

9. _____ Wandering from place to place

10. _____ Reserved

Aloof	Collusion	Efface	Jeopardy
Arable	Conundrum	Emulate	Nomadic
Banal	Cosmopolitan	Impudent	Pernicious
Bashful	Debauch	Inhibit	Pervasive
Clergy	Deplete	Interject	Succinct

Word List #16

11. _____ To imitate

12. _____ To wipe out

13. _____ Puzzle

14. _____ To use up or consume

15. _____ Casually rude

16. _____ Sophisticated

17. _____ Extremely destructive or harmful

18. _____ Marked by compact precision

19. _____ Indulge in immoral behavior

20. _____ Shy

Aloof	Collusion	Efface	Jeopardy
Arable	Conundrum	Emulate	Nomadic
Banal	Cosmopolitan	Impudent	Pernicious
Bashful	Debauch	Inhibit	Pervasive
Clergy	Deplete	Interject	Succinct

Word Scramble #16

1. ADEJOPRY   J _____
2. AFLOO   A _____
3. CILLNOOSU   C _____
4. CEEIJNRTT   I _____
5. AEEIPRSVV   P _____
6. CDMNNORUU   C _____
7. DEEELPT   D _____
8. ACDIMNO   N _____
9. ABFHLSU   B _____
10. CEGLRY   C _____
11. CEIINOPRSU   P _____
12. AEELMTU   E _____
13. ABCDEHU   D _____
14. DEIMNPTU   I _____
15. ACEEFF   E _____
16. BHIIINT   I _____
17. ACILMNOOOPST   C _____
18. AABLN   B _____
19. AABELR   A _____
20. CCCINSTU   S _____

Word Search #16

```
B  M  I  F  K  H  F  V  M  A  G  K  I  I
S  Y  Q  X  G  R  B  J  O  F  I  P  N  J
J  Z  G  Q  E  N  K  I  D  T  C  L  H  F
R  E  T  Z  M  K  O  X  E  W  J  P  I  R
H  D  O  V  U  E  F  M  B  B  V  E  B  D
R  G  F  P  L  Q  K  H  A  M  A  R  I  D
N  H  A  B  A  I  M  P  U  D  E  N  T  E
P  B  A  H  T  R  Y  R  C  F  I  I  A  P
B  R  C  S  E  N  D  H  H  W  M  C  G  L
A  X  O  X  W  N  U  Y  E  A  C  I  X  E
X  F  S  I  U  U  D  E  A  L  O  O  F  T
D  Y  M  N  B  A  S  H  F  U  L  U  E  E
D  C  O  T  S  S  E  S  K  E  L  S  V  T
K  C  P  E  U  J  P  Y  E  F  U  I  P  P
Q  O  O  R  C  I  J  W  U  F  S  J  I  W
F  G  L  J  C  L  P  J  U  A  I  U  X  D
U  G  I  E  I  X  E  P  V  C  O  K  O  S
T  V  T  C  N  D  M  R  N  E  N  E  G  W
I  I  A  T  C  P  E  F  G  U  V  H  D  U
U  F  N  M  T  P  X  C  A  Y  Y  P  L  M
```

Crossword Clues #16

Across

2. Puzzle
3. Spreading widely throughout
6. Indulge in immoral behavior
10. To imitate
11. To wipe out
14. Secret agreement
16. Wandering from place to place
19. Sophisticated

Down

1. A source of danger
2. Members of christian holy orders
4. Suitable for growing crops
5. To use up or consume
7. Marked by compact precision
8. Shy
9. Boring and unoriginal
12. Extremely destructive or harmful
13. To insert between other things
15. Casually rude
17. Reserved
18. To prevent

Crossword Puzzle #16

Word List #17

1. _____ Profuse

2. _____ To exert much effort or energy

3. _____ To esteem

4. _____ Artist's painting surface

5. _____ Out of historical context

6. _____ Fear

7. _____ Supreme ruler or authority

8. _____ To reduce or lessen

9. _____ Inspiring shock

10. _____ A tendency

Abate	Caricature	Inclination	Repose
Adamant	Copious	Maxim	Revere
Anachronistic	Deface	Metamorphosis	Sovereign
Appalling	Enhance	Reconcile	Strain
Canvas	Ignominious	Reiterate	Trepidation

Word List #17

11. _____ To repeat

12. _____ Widely accepted saying

13. _____ Spoil the appearance

14. _____ Come to terms

15. _____ Humiliating

16. _____ Exaggerated portrayal

17. _____ To rest

18. _____ Make better or more attractive

19. _____ The change of form

20. _____ Impervious or stubborn

Abate	Caricature	Inclination	Repose
Adamant	Copious	Maxim	Revere
Anachronistic	Deface	Metamorphosis	Sovereign
Appalling	Enhance	Reconcile	Strain
Canvas	Ignominious	Reiterate	Trepidation

Word Scramble #17

1. ACIIILNNNOT   I _____
2. AIMMX   M _____
3. AEHIMMOOPRSST M _____
4. CCEEILNOR   R _____
5. CIOOPSU   C _____
6. GIIIMNNOOSU   I _____
7. EEOPRS   R _____
8. AACCEIRRTU   C _____
9. AACNSV   C _____
10. EEGINORSV   S _____
11. EEERRV   R _____
12. AINRST   S _____
13. AABET   A _____
14. ACEEHNN   E _____
15. AAGILLNPP   A _____
16. ADEIINOPRTT   T _____
17. AAADMNT   A _____
18. AACCHIINNORST A _____
19. AEEEIRRTT   R _____
20. ACDEEF   D _____

106

Word Search #17

```
R E S T I T U T I O N D A R
T J K M A N D A T E U P M C
C D P D I Q F R L N G U U F
N E O F B T R B P Y Z C I D
M F S Z A N I M A T E D D I
I U O N D T V N X W R H I S
A N H C A J O K E L E C S P
N C T P W C L F T R C U S A
X T M R H U O E C A A N E R
O O O E E V U Q D N L N N A
C K B C K P S S A C I I T G
H Z J I D A I P N I B N I E
M T R P L Y T D T R G M M M
D D E I T K O T I W A U P I
D I S C O M F I T K T E A X
U M Y E O B G D H P E X S K
C O B S T R E P E R O U S K
C K W M S A G I S B R Z I L
K D I M I N U T I V E C V B
K N Q J X V L I S O R Y E R
```

Crossword Clues #17

Across

1. Widely accepted saying
4. To reduce or lessen
6. Make better or more attractive
8. Artist's painting surface
10. The change of form
14. To esteem
15. A tendency
18. Supreme ruler or authority
19. Out of historical context

Down

2. Impervious or stubborn
3. To rest
5. Inspiring shock
7. Exaggerated portrayal
9. Spoil the appearance
11. To repeat
12. To exert much effort or energy
13. Fear
15. Humiliating
16. Profuse
17. Come to terms

Crossword Puzzle #17

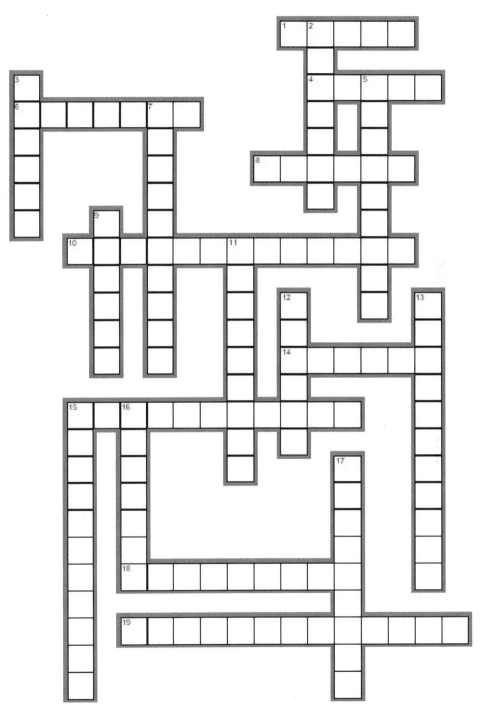

Word List #18

1. _____ To set

2. _____ To reject

3. _____ Something that baffles understanding

4. _____ Dull

5. _____ To increase or make greater

6. _____ Excessively bold

7. _____ Forbidden

8. _____ To add to

9. _____ Self-satisfied ignorance of danger

10 _____ Greatly distressing

Aggrandize	Canny	Enigma	Modulate
Audacious	Chronicle	Harrowing	Nocturnal
Augment	Complacency	Illicit	Parody
Buffet	Debacle	Inane	Repudiate
Calibrate	Desolate	Insipid	Retract

Word List #18

11. _____ Relating to or occurring during the night

12. _____ Silly and meaningless

13. _____ A disastrous failure

14. _____ To pass from one state to another

15. _____ Shrewd

16. _____ Withdraw

17. _____ A satirical imitation

18. _____ Deserted

19. _____ A written history

20. _____ To strike with force

Aggrandize	Canny	Enigma	Modulate
Audacious	Chronicle	Harrowing	Nocturnal
Augment	Complacency	Illicit	Parody
Buffet	Debacle	Inane	Repudiate
Calibrate	Desolate	Insipid	Retract

Word Scramble #18

1. ADELMOTU   M _____
2. ACNNY   C _____
3. ACCCELMNOPY   C _____
4. ABCDEEL   D _____
5. BEFFTU   B _____
6. CIIILLT   I _____
7. ADEELOST   D _____
8. ADOPRY   P _____
9. ACERRTT   R _____
10. AABCEILRT   C _____
11. AGHINORRW   H _____
12. AADEGGINRZ   A _____
13. AEGMNTU   A _____
14. AEINN   I _____
15. AACDIOSUU   A _____
16. CCEHILNOR   C _____
17. AEGIMN   E _____
18. DIIINPS   I _____
19. ADEEIPRTU   R _____
20. ACLNNORTU   N _____

Word Search #18

```
P  J  A  T  V  J  P  K  Q  V  Z  F  M  F
C  A  G  G  R  A  N  D  I  Z  E  W  C  L
W  U  R  E  P  U  D  I  A  T  E  B  E  M
B  D  V  O  M  N  Y  K  A  R  P  G  S  D
C  A  F  M  D  T  I  B  G  T  P  L  I  D
P  C  M  O  O  Y  F  N  E  N  E  L  L  V
A  I  H  X  I  D  I  H  S  T  I  F  L  G
H  O  K  R  F  W  U  J  A  Z  F  S  I  M
J  U  C  C  O  M  P  L  A  C  E  N  C  Y
W  S  C  R  U  N  O  J  A  C  L  S  I  C
J  L  R  I  Y  S  I  I  U  T  W  O  T  A
W  A  E  O  E  I  K  C  V  K  E  X  C  L
H  O  T  D  E  B  A  C  L  E  B  B  A  I
T  J  R  K  B  E  J  T  N  E  B  U  N  B
W  B  A  Q  J  B  Q  A  V  N  W  F  N  R
N  O  C  T  U  R  N  A  L  I  O  F  Y  A
I  W  T  W  I  I  Z  A  U  G  M  E  N  T
Q  I  V  C  R  K  C  N  S  M  Z  T  O  E
S  Q  T  B  R  F  C  P  W  A  L  S  G  F
I  N  S  I  P  I  D  U  Y  N  N  G  B  B
```

Crossword Clues #18

Across

3. Relating to or occurring during the night
5. Self-satisfied ignorance of danger
6. Withdraw
9. Deserted
12. To increase or make greater
17. Forbidden
18. To reject
19. Excessively bold
20. A disastrous failure

Down

1. Silly and meaningless
2. A satirical imitation
4. To set
7. Shrewd
8. To strike with force
10. Something that baffles understanding
11. A written history
13. To add to
14. Dull
15. To pass from one state to another
16. Greatly distressing

Crossword Puzzle #18

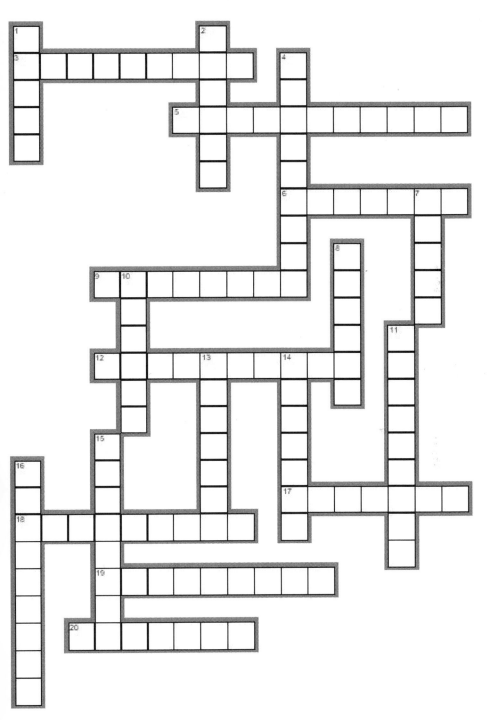

Word List #19

1. _____ Intensity of emotion

2. _____ Having a lying

3. _____ A side-by-side position

4. _____ Spread out

5. _____ Rude

6. _____ To absorb

7. _____ To improve

8. _____ Excessively showy

9. _____ Intimidating

10. _____ Bruise

Ameliorate	Fervor	Juxtaposition	Placate
Chronological	Immerse	Maudlin	Primordial
Contusion	Ingenious	Mendacious	Propagate
Daunting	Ingratiate	Ostensible	Pugnacious
Duplicity	Insolent	Ostentatious	Truncate

Word List #19

11. _____ Clever

12. _____ Arranged in order of time

13. _____ Crafty dishonesty

14 _____ Original

15. _____ To ease the anger of

16. _____ To shorten by cutting off

17. _____ Weakly sentimental

18. _____ Gain favor through flattery

19. _____ Quarrelsome

20. _____ Appearing as such

Ameliorate	Fervor	Juxtaposition	Placate
Chronological	Immerse	Maudlin	Primordial
Contusion	Ingenious	Mendacious	Propagate
Daunting	Ingratiate	Ostensible	Pugnacious
Duplicity	Insolent	Ostentatious	Truncate

Word Scramble #19

1. AAEEILMORT   A _____
2. ADILMNU   M _____
3. EGIINNOSU   I _____
4. EFORRV   F _____
5. CDIILPTUY   D _____
6. ADGINNTU   D _____
7. AEINOOSSTTTU   O _____
8. ACCGHILLNOOOR   C _____
9. ACENRTTU   T _____
10. ADIILMOPRR   P _____
11. ACDEIMNOSU   M _____
12. EILNNOST   I _____
13. EEIMMRS   I _____
14. AAEGIINRTT   I _____
15. AIIJNOOPSTTUX   J _____
16. AAEGOPPRT   P _____
17. CINNOOSTU   C _____
18. AACELPT   P _____
19. BEEILNOSST   O _____
20. ACGINOPSUU   P _____

Word Search #19

```
R  C  V  L  G  J  D  K  U  Q  A  G  K  C
J  Z  S  B  P  L  A  C  A  T  E  H  W  H
G  O  S  T  E  N  T  A  T  I  O  U  S  R
R  K  V  W  K  K  S  D  S  Q  L  N  H  O
Z  P  R  I  M  O  R  D  I  A  L  J  Y  N
L  M  E  N  D  A  C  I  O  U  S  T  S  O
Q  A  Y  G  P  G  Q  N  D  F  I  U  Y  L
H  U  G  R  Q  L  P  A  N  C  O  J  U  O
E  D  R  A  J  H  G  O  I  I  S  U  Z  G
A  L  V  T  Q  Z  I  L  C  M  T  X  S  I
E  I  E  I  R  S  A  P  M  E  T  M  C
Z  N  L  A  U  U  N  A  R  E  N  A  N  A
I  C  F  T  D  G  N  D  O  R  S  P  R  L
P  N  N  E  U  P  D  C  P  S  I  O  G  Q
X  O  S  P  R  C  E  B  A  E  B  S  R  C
C  Q  R  O  I  V  P  Q  G  T  L  I  B  F
Q  A  M  E  L  I  O  R  A  T  E  T  X  T
Q  R  V  Z  A  E  L  R  T  H  V  I  Q  Y
N  X  C  P  C  I  N  G  E  N  I  O  U  S
F  B  Q  D  A  U  N  T  I  N  G  N  B  X
```

Crossword Clues #19

Across

2. Crafty dishonesty
5. Clever
7. Arranged in order of time
9. To absorb
10. A side-by-side position
14. Having a lying
17. Intensity of emotion
20. Intimidating

Down

1. Quarrelsome
3. Rude
4. To ease the anger of
6. Bruise
8. Original
11. Excessively showy
12. Appearing as such
13. Gain favor through flattery
15. To improve
16. Spread out
18. To shorten by cutting off
19. Weakly sentimental

Crossword Puzzle #19

Word List #20

1. _____ To demolish

2. _____ Real or genuine

3. _____ Natural liking or attraction

4. _____ Delight greatly in

5. _____ Having no personal preference

6. _____ Distinctly dissimilar or unlike

7. _____ Heavenly

8. _____ A system with ranked groups

9. _____ Friendly and peaceable

10. _____ Learned

Affinity	Corrosive	Efficacious	Neutral
Amicable	Counteract	Erudite	Palpable
Appraise	Didactic	Ethereal	Raze
Authentic	Diverse	Hierarchy	Resignation
Biased	Effervescent	Licentious	Wallow

Word List #20

11. _____ Unfairly prejudiced

12. _____ The act of giving up

13. _____ Intended to instruct

14 _____ Lacking moral restraint

15. _____ Bubbly

16. _____ Capable of being perceived

17. _____ To assess the worth or value of

18. _____ To neutralize

19. _____ Effective

20. _____ Tending to erode

Affinity	Corrosive	Efficacious	Neutral
Amicable	Counteract	Erudite	Palpable
Appraise	Didactic	Ethereal	Raze
Authentic	Diverse	Hierarchy	Resignation
Biased	Effervescent	Licentious	Wallow

Word Scramble #20

1. AEGIINNORST   R _____
2. CEIILNOSTU   L _____
3. AEEEHLRT   E _____
4. AABELLPP   P _____
5. ACEHINTTU   A _____
6. AAEIPPRS   A _____
7. ACCENORTTU   C _____
8. ACCDDIIT   D _____
9. DEEIRSV   D _____
10. AERZ   R _____
11. ACEHHIRRY   H _____
12. CEIOORRSV   C _____
13. ABDEIS   B _____
14. DEEIRTU   E _____
15. AFFIINTY   A _____
16. AELNRTU   N _____
17. ACCEFFIIOSU   E _____
18. CEEEEFFNRSTV   E _____
19. AABCEILM   A _____
20. ALLOWW   W _____

Word Search #20

```
O  I  F  M  M  J  A  P  P  R  A  I  S  E
U  W  R  C  O  U  N  T  E  R  A  C  T  R
Y  E  F  F  E  R  V  E  S  C  E  N  T  Z
P  M  A  Z  E  W  L  N  U  T  H  D  D  K
A  M  I  C  A  B  L  E  I  T  E  I  E  I
W  W  Y  F  A  L  H  D  P  S  R  D  D  M
F  A  B  P  W  M  U  H  A  D  E  A  H  S
J  A  L  G  P  R  Z  I  V  O  S  C  L  W
W  A  V  L  E  W  B  E  D  W  I  T  G  L
P  C  D  R  O  T  E  R  D  E  G  I  X  I
P  O  N  D  A  W  I  A  S  P  N  C  C  C
B  R  N  M  T  Z  N  R  P  N  A  I  W  E
W  R  D  E  H  X  E  C  U  F  T  M  I  N
C  O  I  Q  K  V  M  H  G  N  I  G  C  T
H  S  S  I  I  F  S  Y  E  E  O  F  R  I
Q  I  O  D  L  J  V  H  I  H  N  H  A  O
G  V  T  B  W  E  T  H  E  R  E  A  L  U
W  E  K  Y  L  U  H  L  U  R  E  P  G  S
G  Q  F  X  A  F  F  I  N  I  T  Y  F  R
E  Z  Y  E  F  F  I  C  A  C  I  O  U  S
```

Crossword Clues #20

Across

4. Distinctly dissimilar or unlike
8. To demolish
9. Real or genuine
11. Having no personal preference
13. The act of giving up
17. Tending to erode
18. Lacking moral restraint
19. Capable of being perceived
20. Heavenly

Down

1. Unfairly prejudiced
2. Friendly and peaceable
3. Intended to instruct
5. Learned
6. To neutralize
7. To assess the worth or value of
10. Effective
12. Bubbly
14. Natural liking or attraction
15. Delight greatly in
16. A system with ranked groups

Crossword Puzzle #20

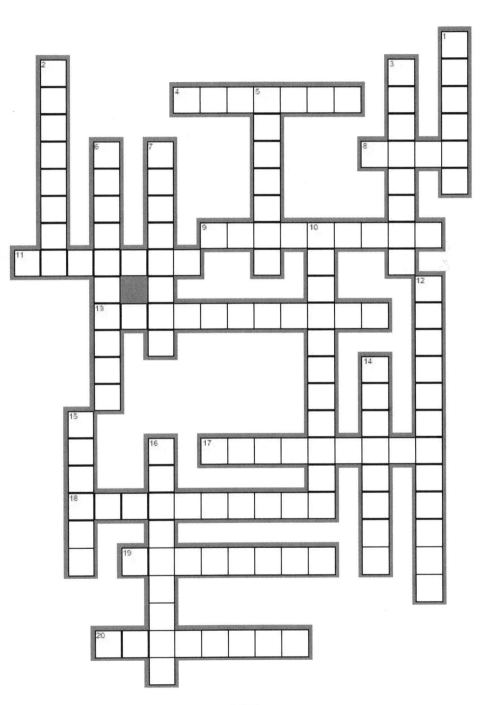

Word List #21

1. _____ Burdensome

2. _____ Unbiased and impartial

3. _____ To stop

4. _____ Shy

5. _____ To perceive

6. _____ Wanting harm to befall others

7. _____ Motivated by irrational enthusiasm

8. _____ To move in waves

9. _____ Drawn to the company of others

10. _____ Enduring pain without complaint

Abet	Diffident	Fanatic	Objective
Abscond	Discern	Gregarious	Onerous
Advocate	Elaborate	Heresy	Resolve
Balk	Empathy	Incumbent	Stoic
Capacious	Ennui	Malevolent	Undulate

Word List #21

11. _____ Understanding another's feelings

12. _____ Encourage or assist wrongdoing

13. _____ To sneak away and hide

14 _____ Boredom

15. _____ To argue in favor of something

16. _____ Determination or firmness

17. _____ Currently holding an office

18. _____ Very spacious

19. _____ Against orthodox beliefs

20. _____ Complex

Abet	Diffident	Fanatic	Objective
Abscond	Discern	Gregarious	Onerous
Advocate	Elaborate	Heresy	Resolve
Balk	Empathy	Incumbent	Stoic
Capacious	Ennui	Malevolent	Undulate

Word Scramble #21

1. EELORSV   R _____
2. BCEEIJOTV   O _____
3. EEHRSY   H _____
4. AEELLMNOTV   M _____
5. CDEINRS   D _____
6. AABEELORT   E _____
7. ABET   A _____
8. CIOST   S _____
9. AACDEOTV   A _____
10. ABKL   B _____
11. ENOORSU   O _____
12. DDEFFIINT   D _____
13. AEHMPTY   E _____
14. AEGGIORRSU   G _____
15. EINNU   E _____
16. ABCDNOS   A _____
17. ADELNTUU   U _____
18. BCEIMNNTU   I _____
19. AACFINT   F _____
20. AACCIOPSU   C _____

Word Search #21

```
B R V T N D W L C N Q P L U
Z Y Y G R E G A R I O U S B
O P M J L U F O U N E U Z E
B M O F Y I A N K C M O K S
N W B E D Z N E T U P L A N
T R J I O E A R L M A D W D
A V E K S S T O F B T B Z C
N Z C U Y W I U P E H I F A
X S T O I C C S B N Y H M P
B D I F F I D E N T T E X A
O I V V M W T L S C T R L C
L S E T X A A A P A C E X I
M C A W L A H B C V F S P O
A E R U Z B Q O E E J Y D U
Q R D E J Q V R U T J C H S
O N F V S D M A B S C O N D
U Y N B A O G T X I U R V E
B B E G M A L E V O L E N T
O H N W L G O V T I U J G V
S U E L Q E V X E S N U B S
```

Crossword Clues #21

Across

3. To move in waves
6. Very spacious
7. Motivated by irrational enthusiasm
9. Determination or firmness
11. Enduring pain without complaint
13. Drawn to the company of others
14. To argue in favor of something
16. To perceive
19. Encourage or assist wrongdoing

Down

1. Boredom
2. Currently holding an office
4. Complex
5. To stop
8. To sneak away and hide
10. Burdensome
12. Wanting harm to befall others
15. Unbiased and impartial
16. Shy
17. Understanding another's feelings
18. Against orthodox beliefs

Crossword Puzzle #21

Word List #22

1. _____ Challenger of norms

2. _____ Robust

3. _____ To put down

4. _____ Gloomy or sullen

5. _____ Gaudy

6. _____ Charmingly old-fashioned

7. _____ Contrary to expectations

8. _____ Basic and fundamental

9. _____ Resentment

10. _____ Noble

Belittle	Gullible	Jocular	Stringent
Cognizant	Hardy	Magnanimous	Tirade
Corroborate	Iconoclast	Morose	Transient
Denigrate	Intrinsic	Propensity	Umbrage
Garish	Ironic	Quaint	Vagrant

Word List #22

11. _____ Wanderer without home

12. _____ Aware

13. _____ A speech of violent denunciation

14. _____ Lasting a very short time

15. _____ Humorous or playful

16. _____ Easily deceived or fooled

17. _____ Strict or precise

18. _____ To belittle

19. _____ An inclination

20. _____ To support with evidence

Belittle	Gullible	Jocular	Stringent
Cognizant	Hardy	Magnanimous	Tirade
Corroborate	Iconoclast	Morose	Transient
Denigrate	Intrinsic	Propensity	Umbrage
Garish	Ironic	Quaint	Vagrant

Word Scramble #22

1. ACGINNOTZ   C _____
2. BEGILLLU   G _____
3. EGINNRSTT   S _____
4. ADEIRT   T _____
5. AEINNRSTT   T _____
6. ACCILNOOST   I _____
7. ABCEOOORRRT   C _____
8. CIINOR   I _____
9. ABEGMRU   U _____
10. EINOPPRSTY   P _____
11. CIIINNRST   I _____
12. AINQTU   Q _____
13. BEEILLTT   B _____
14. ADEEGINRT   D _____
15. ACJLORU   J _____
16. AAGNRTV   V _____
17. ADHRY   H _____
18. AGHIRS   G _____
19. AAGIMMNNOSU   M _____
20. EMOORS   M _____

Word Search #22

```
O D X O U W B V O A A U E I
A K Z Y V V T D P Z X W W S
F Q H T Y J D J R G D C U X
M I E F B O V N O A U O J A
A E E B T C E O P R M R R D
M B S E E U L K E I B R E A
R O T X R L K O N S R O V B
X T R L A A I A S H A B L N
B R I O V R N T I G G O C S
T A N R S G Z F T U E R O U
Z N G W A E Y N Y L D A G S
S S E M L D A L I L E T N T
B I N U R R E B R I N E I E
S E T A G M I I O B I M Z H
K N H A K Z N Y N L G D A T
D T V H R M W K I E R H N F
F P F I C O N O C L A S T D
Z F F Z U Q U A I N T T H V
G I Y F S I L J O G E G A T
Y O E U I N T R I N S I C G
```

Crossword Clues #22

Across

7. Basic and fundamental
8. Resentment
10. Charmingly old-fashioned
11. Aware
13. Gloomy or sullen
15. Strict or precise
17. To belittle
19. An inclination
20. To put down

Down

1. Easily deceived or fooled
2. Wanderer without home
3. Challenger of norms
4. Humorous or playful
5. To support with evidence
6. Noble
9. A speech of violent denunciation
12. Contrary to expectations
14. Robust
16. Lasting a very short time
18. Gaudy

Crossword Puzzle #22

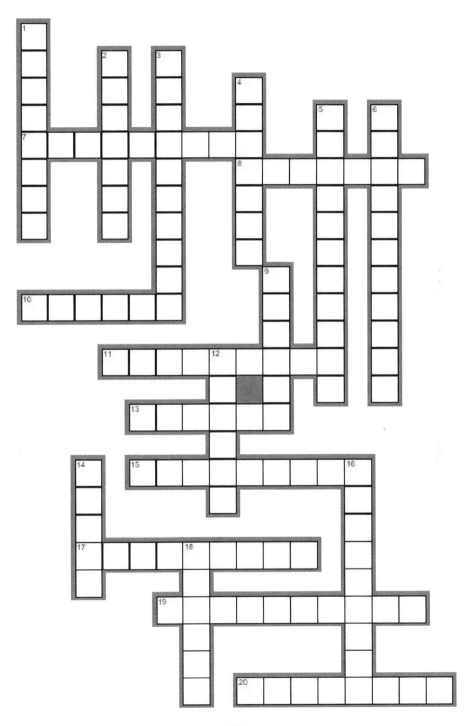

Word List #23

1. _____ Small or miniature

2. _____ To criticize or speak ill of

3. _____ Noisy

4. _____ To cheat

5. _____ Traveling from place to place

6. _____ Compensation for loss

7. _____ Brave in the face of danger

8. _____ Adjust for accuracy

9. _____ To thwart

10. _____ No longer used or existing

Animated	Defunct	Frivolous	Obstreperous
Antithesis	Diminutive	Impassive	Precipice
Bilk	Discomfit	Intrepid	Rancid
Compatible	Disparage	Itinerant	Recalibrate
Cunning	Dissent	Mandate	Restitution

Word List #23

11. _____ Sly

12. _____ To disagree

13. _____ Foul-smelling or stale

14. _____ An authoritative command

15. _____ Agreeable

16. _____ The absolute opposite

17. _____ The face of a cliff

18. _____ Of little importance

19. _____ Stoic

20. _____ Lively

Animated	Defunct	Frivolous	Obstreperous
Antithesis	Diminutive	Impassive	Precipice
Bilk	Discomfit	Intrepid	Rancid
Compatible	Disparage	Itinerant	Recalibrate
Cunning	Dissent	Mandate	Restitution

141

Word Scramble #23

1. AEHIINSSTT   A _____
2. AADEIMNT   A _____
3. BEEOOPRRSSTU   O _____
4. DEIIIMNTUV   D _____
5. ACDINR   R _____
6. CDEFNTU   D _____
7. CCEEIIPPR   P _____
8. DEINSST   D _____
9. AABCEEILRRT   R _____
10. AEIINNRTT   I _____
11. ABCEILMOPT   C _____
12. AADEGIPRS   D _____
13. CDFIIMOST   D _____
14. FILOORSUV   F _____
15. AADEMNT   M _____
16. EIINORSTTTU   R _____
17. AEIIMPSSV   I _____
18. DEIINPRT   I _____
19. BIKL   B _____
20. CGINNNU   C _____

Word Search #23

```
R  E  S  T  I  T  U  T  I  O  N  D  A  R
T  J  K  M  A  N  D  A  T  E  U  P  M  C
C  D  P  D  I  Q  F  R  L  N  G  U  U  F
N  E  O  F  B  T  R  B  P  Y  Z  C  I  D
M  F  S  Z  A  N  I  M  A  T  E  D  D  I
I  U  O  N  T  V  N  X  W  R  H  I  S
A  N  H  C  A  J  O  K  E  L  E  C  S  P
N  C  T  P  W  C  L  F  T  R  C  U  S  A
X  T  M  R  H  U  O  E  C  A  A  N  E  R
O  O  O  E  E  V  U  Q  D  N  L  N  N  A
C  K  B  C  K  P  S  S  A  C  I  I  T  G
H  Z  J  I  D  A  I  P  N  I  B  N  I  E
M  T  R  P  L  Y  T  D  T  D  R  G  M  M
D  D  E  I  T  K  O  T  I  W  A  U  P  I
D  I  S  C  O  M  F  I  T  K  T  E  A  X
U  M  Y  E  O  B  G  D  H  P  E  X  S  K
C  O  B  S  T  R  E  P  E  R  O  U  S  K
C  K  W  M  S  A  G  I  S  B  R  Z  I  L
K  D  I  M  I  N  U  T  I  V  E  C  V  B
K  N  Q  J  X  V  L  I  S  O  R  Y  E  R
```

Crossword Clues #23

Across

1. Adjust for accuracy
3. Of little importance
4. The face of a cliff
5. To criticize or speak ill of
9. The absolute opposite
10. Brave in the face of danger
12. Sly
17. Compensation for loss
18. Small or miniature
19. An authoritative command

Down

2. Traveling from place to place
5. No longer used or existing
6. Agreeable
7. Noisy
8. To disagree
11. To thwart
13. Stoic
14. Foul-smelling or stale
15. To cheat
16. Lively

Crossword Puzzle #23

Word List #24

1. _____ To long for

2. _____ Secondary or subordinate

3. _____ Applicable to all

4. _____ Unconventional, odd person

5. _____ Ardent

6. _____ Hold back to a later time

7. _____ To go underwater

8. _____ Marked by extreme conservatism

9. _____ So old that it is no longer useful

10. _____ Diverse

Adroit	Atone	Fervent	Refute
Anecdote	Coherent	Infamy	Subjugate
Antiquated	Debunk	Manifold	Submerge
Arcane	Defer	Prevalent	Subsidiary
Aspire	Eccentric	Reactionary	Universal

Word List #24

11. _____ To prove wrong

12. _____ Short account of an incident

13. _____ Notoriety

14 _____ To repent

15. _____ Logically consistent

16. _____ Commonly occurring

17. _____ Skillful

18. _____ Expose false claims

19. _____ To bring under control

20. _____ Obscure

Adroit	Atone	Fervent	Refute
Anecdote	Coherent	Infamy	Subjugate
Antiquated	Debunk	Manifold	Submerge
Arcane	Defer	Prevalent	Subsidiary
Aspire	Eccentric	Reactionary	Universal

147

Word Scramble #24

1. AFIMNY   I _____
2. EEFNRTV   F _____
3. ADFILMNO   M _____
4. ACDEENOT   A _____
5. AACENR   A _____
6. ABEGJSTUU   S _____
7. CEEHNORT   C _____
8. DEEFR   D _____
9. AEILNRSUV   U _____
10. AEELNPRTV   P _____
11. AEIPRS   A _____
12. BEEGMRSU   S _____
13. BDEKNU   D _____
14. CCCEEINRT   E _____
15. ABDIIRSSUY   S _____
16. AADEINQTTU   A _____
17. AACEINORRTY R _____
18. AENOT   A _____
19. ADIORT   A _____
20. EEFRTU   R _____

Word Search #24

```
H  K  V  J  T  A  P  J  M  P  U  Y  S  X
H  W  R  D  N  O  J  A  A  S  R  K  T  B
U  R  E  A  C  T  I  O  N  A  R  Y  N  K
N  E  F  X  A  D  R  O  I  T  Y  T  H  X
B  E  R  T  O  X  Y  D  F  M  U  D  K  P
A  F  P  B  C  O  I  N  O  D  E  D  C  C
O  E  X  R  U  S  P  F  L  P  E  I  B  O
E  R  K  W  B  T  D  Z  D  T  R  F  Y  H
P  V  S  U  B  J  U  G  A  T  E  Y  E  E
W  E  S  U  V  C  U  U  N  Y  U  K  E  R
A  N  Y  Y  J  X  Q  E  J  Y  N  R  C  E
C  T  I  L  P  I  C  T  A  U  I  P  G  N
K  I  O  A  T  C  K  B  B  P  V  R  N  T
Z  N  V  N  E  T  C  E  S  X  E  E  J  G
Q  F  A  E  E  B  D  A  Z  M  R  V  C  G
T  A  R  C  A  N  E  S  B  B  S  A  U  Y
T  M  V  D  F  I  F  U  D  B  A  L  H  O
I  Y  O  O  G  Y  S  F  O  U  L  E  G  V
H  A  W  T  A  P  C  H  I  Y  Z  N  W  O
T  N  R  E  F  U  T  E  Z  B  Q  T  O  W
```

Crossword Clues #24

Across

3. Obscure
4. To prove wrong
6. To repent
7. Notoriety
10. Expose false claims
11. Applicable to all
13. To go underwater
16. Skillful
17. Hold back to a later time
19. To bring under control
20. Diverse

Down

1. Logically consistent
2. Unconventional, odd person
5. Marked by extreme conservatism
8. Ardent
9. Secondary or subordinate
12. Short account of an incident
14. So old that it is no longer useful
15. Commonly occurring
18. To long for

Crossword Puzzle #24

Word List #25

1. _____ Scold or counsel

2. _____ Small and of little importance

3. _____ Insignificant; of a small amount

4. _____ Vaguely defined

5. _____ Extremely poisonous or injurious

6. _____ Expressive

7. _____ Overbearing pride

8. _____ A perfect example

9. _____ An angry verbal attack

10. _____ Hoarder of wealth

Admonish	Arrogant	Miser	Reticent
Abrogate	Eloquent	Nebulous	Trivial
Accolade	Epitome	Paltry	Uncanny
Agile	Erratic	Prudent	Virulent
Amity	Invective	Rescind	Zealous

Word List #25

11. _____ To take back

12. _____ Unpredictable or unusual

13. _____ Moving quickly and lightly

14 _____ Form of praise or an award

15. _____ Revoke formally

16. _____ Reserved or silent

17. _____ Strangely unsettling or mysterious

18. _____ Friendly relations

19. _____ Fervent

20. _____ Cautious

Admonish	Arrogant	Miser	Reticent
Abrogate	Eloquent	Nebulous	Trivial
Accolade	Epitome	Paltry	Uncanny
Agile	Erratic	Prudent	Virulent
Amity	Invective	Rescind	Zealous

Word Scramble #25

1. AIMTY   A _____
2. EILNRTUV   V _____
3. EELNOQTU   E _____
4. AEGIL   A _____
5. AIILRTV   T _____
6. CEEIINTVV   I _____
7. AELOSUZ   Z _____
8. ALPRTY   P _____
9. ACEIRRT   E _____
10. AACCDELO   A _____
11. EEIMOPT   E _____
12. ADHIMNOS   A _____
13. DENPRTU   P _____
14. CDEINRS   R _____
15. BELNOSUU   N _____
16. AABEGORT   A _____
17. CEEINRTT   R _____
18. EIMRS   M _____
19. AAGNORRT   A _____
20. ACNNNUY   U _____

Word Search #25

```
C Z Q B E R R A T I C N S C
Y H E M G T M D S P Q T A R
A Q Z A T J D M Y L L U P N
V R G J L S D O F Y G A N G
T E R M D O K N T R B C F E
Q T A O N Y U I E E Y C M L
L I T J G P M S P S G O T O
M C D C H A I H U C T L I Q
I E U J M N O R I Z A N U
J N N U O J L T P N K D V E
G T C A A U T E Y D P E E N
D W A I B G H X H K A X C T
V Q N E T R I V I A L C T B
X T N D W M O L T K T E I M
E T Y Q K G G G E G R Z V O
N F A K L S Y M A O Y V E R
J M V I R U L E N T S R P B
P Q R X R W P R U D E N T P
M Z C R W R A E Y G C X B N
I K Y A F O N D R B Y V E Q
```

Crossword Clues #25

Across

1. Strangely unsettling or mysterious
4. Fervent
8. Overbearing pride
9. Cautious
12. Unpredictable or unusual
14. An angry verbal attack
15. Form of praise or an award
18. Expressive
19. Friendly relations

Down

2. Vaguely defined
3. Revoke formally
5. A perfect example
6. Extremely poisonous or injurious
7. Reserved or silent
10. To take back
11. Small and of little importance
13. Hoarder of wealth
16. Scold or counsel
17. Insignificant; of a small amount
19. Moving quickly and lightly

Crossword Puzzle #25

Word List #26

1. _____ Openly straightforward and direct

2. _____ To sharpen

3. _____ Pushy

4. _____ Conflict

5. _____ Extremely joyful

6. _____ To condemn

7. _____ Self-denying and austere

8. _____ Fertile

9. _____ To render incomprehensible

10. _____ Extremely sharp or intense

Abdicate	Brusque	Fathom	Protean
Acumen	Candid	Fecund	Reclusive
Acute	Condone	Obfuscate	Sensuous
Affluent	Convene	Obtrusive	Strife
Ascetic	Exuberant	Proscribe	Whet

Word List #26

11. _____ Appealing to the senses

12. _____ Solitary

13. _____ To pardon

14 _____ To call together

15. _____ To give up, such as power or duty

16. _____ Keen insight

17. _____ To understand

18. _____ Versatile or adaptable

19. _____ Wealthy or prosperous

20. _____ Short

Abdicate	Brusque	Fathom	Protean
Acumen	Candid	Fecund	Reclusive
Acute	Condone	Obfuscate	Sensuous
Affluent	Convene	Obtrusive	Strife
Ascetic	Exuberant	Proscribe	Whet

Word Scramble #26

1. ACCEIST   A _____
2. AENOPRT   P _____
3. CDENNOO   C _____
4. AEFFLNTU   A _____
5. AABCDEIT   A _____
6. CEENNOV   C _____
7. ENOSSSUU   S _____
8. AFHMOT   F _____
9. BCEIOPRRS   P _____
10. EHTW   W _____
11. ACETU   A _____
12. CDEFNU   F _____
13. ACDDIN   C _____
14. ACEMNU   A _____
15. ABCEFOSTU   O _____
16. BEIORSTUV   O _____
17. CEEILRSUV   R _____
18. ABEENRTUX   E _____
19. BEQRSUU   B _____
20. EFIRST   S _____

Word Search #26

```
E  L  M  W  L  F  T  S  K  T  L  P  H  V
H  X  O  Y  K  W  S  V  U  A  V  E  G  G
D  C  U  A  Z  S  V  C  Z  C  Y  K  Q  V
A  Y  U  B  C  C  E  O  M  G  C  E  U  F
Y  Q  Y  D  E  U  P  N  Q  B  O  R  L  T
R  Z  E  I  L  R  T  V  S  R  N  E  R  R
F  Y  Q  C  P  L  A  E  Y  U  D  C  L  M
J  L  P  A  Q  S  C  N  X  S  O  L  M  C
Q  J  R  T  O  I  A  E  T  Q  N  U  W  B
Z  H  O  E  T  E  Q  F  M  U  E  S  S  I
J  G  S  E  T  K  Y  F  E  E  F  I  E  J
T  V  C  O  M  W  V  F  D  O  G  V  I  S
P  S  R  B  E  I  I  I  A  B  W  E  S  Z
A  P  I  F  Q  R  D  B  Q  T  W  Q  P  Q
R  X  B  U  T  N  I  K  C  R  H  C  O  F
C  K  E  S  A  F  K  O  O  U  E  O  S  G
D  F  E  C  U  N  D  M  S  S  T  Q  M  S
H  S  L  A  C  U  M  E  N  I  X  Q  Q  K
P  J  I  T  P  Q  O  R  V  V  M  B  U  S
R  C  Q  E  A  F  F  L  U  E  N  T  E  Z
```

Crossword Clues #26

Across

2. Conflict
5. To pardon
6. To render incomprehensible
7. Self-denying and austere
11. To give up, such as power or duty
14. Solitary
15. Appealing to the senses
16. Keen insight
18. Fertile
19. Extremely sharp or intense

Down

1. Versatile or adaptable
3. To condemn
4. To sharpen
8. Extremely joyful
9. Short
10. Pushy
12. To call together
13. Wealthy or prosperous
17. Openly straightforward and direct
18. To understand

Crossword Puzzle #26

Word List #27

1. _____ Friendly and approachable

2. _____ Mercy

3. _____ Exclusion from a group

4. _____ Serious and dignified

5. _____ A person who agitates

6. _____ Appropriate or applicable

7. _____ Showing care in doing one's work

8. _____ Extremely skilled

9. _____ An item that increases comfort

10. _____ Being born or beginning

Abduct	Clemency	Exhort	Palliate
Adept	Commensurate	Fastidious	Relevant
Affable	Diligent	Incendiary	Skeptical
Amenity	Effulgent	Nascent	Solemn
Caucus	Excavate	Ostracism	Temper

Word List #27

11. _____ Moderate or restrain

12. _____ To kidnap

13. _____ Giving careful attention to detail

14. _____ To urge

15. _____ Corresponding in size or amount

16. _____ Dig up or uncover

17. _____ Doubting

18. _____ To reduce the severity of

19. _____ A closed political meeting

20. _____ Radiant

Abduct	Clemency	Exhort	Palliate
Adept	Commensurate	Fastidious	Relevant
Affable	Diligent	Incendiary	Skeptical
Amenity	Effulgent	Nascent	Solemn
Caucus	Excavate	Ostracism	Temper

Word Scramble #27

1. EEFFGLNTU   E _____
2. ACENNST   N _____
3. EEMPRT   T _____
4. ADFIIOSSTU   F _____
5. AACEETVX   E _____
6. ACEIKLPST   S _____
7. AEIMNTY   A _____
8. ACDEIINNRY   I _____
9. AABEFFL   A _____
10. ACIMORSST   O _____
11. ADEPT   A _____
12. ACEEMMNORSTU   C _____
13. CCEELMNY   C _____
14. DEGIILNT   D _____
15. ABCDTU   A _____
16. EHORTX   E _____
17. ELMNOS   S _____
18. AEELNRTV   R _____
19. ACCSUU   C _____
20. AAEILLPT   P _____

Word Search #27

```
P O J Q G M A G T V J X M N
V S N Y T Z S P U T Y L M T
Q T S S H M E O C B W Y R E
H R K D O D B I L V A O P M
H A E I A L Q X E M H D P P
O C P L M B E I M X A S O E
E I T I E O D M E F Q C M R
X S I G N V X U N A J O L D
X M C E I C A A C S P M Y A
M E A N T A E N Y T A M Z L
P L L T Y U X N T I L E F Z
M J L J V C C A D D L N I Q
I W D P P U A S X I I S J M
G M J D Y S V C K O A U W R
G S X A Y Q A E D U T R S P
M O S F E D T N C S E A Y P
T C H T L I E T C C S T S Z
G H G P P A F F A B L E R F
Q X I R S S L Z C J Q H B I
G O E I E F F U L G E N T P
```

Crossword Clues #27

Across

2. Giving careful attention to detail
6. Extremely skilled
8. Appropriate or applicable
9. Friendly and approachable
13. A closed political meeting
15. Dig up or uncover
19. An item that increases comfort
20. Radiant

Down

1. Showing care in doing one's work
3. A person who agitates
4. To reduce the severity of
5. Being born or beginning
7. Mercy
10. To kidnap
11. Exclusion from a group
12. Serious and dignified
14. Corresponding in size or amount
16. To urge
17. Doubting
18. Moderate or restrain

Crossword Puzzle #27

Word List #28

1. _____ To laugh at mockingly

2. _____ To belittle

3. _____ A perplexed

4. _____ Weaken gradually or secretly

5. _____ A person without moral scruples

6. _____ Having a lack of concern

7. _____ Friendly

8. _____ To list

9. _____ Concerned

10. _____ A violent commotion or disturbance

Catalog	Disrepute	Maelstrom	Reprobate
Contravene	Fickle	Nonchalant	Simian
Delineate	Genial	Opulent	Solicitous
Deprecate	Haughty	Proficient	Strenuous
Deride	Inquisitive	Quandary	Undermine

Word List #28

11. _____ Curious

12. _____ Changeable or unpredictable

13. _____ Rich and superior in quality

14. _____ Apelike

15. _____ Disdainfully proud

16. _____ Loss of good reputation

17. _____ Requiring great effort

18. _____ To describe

19. _____ To contradict

20. _____ Skilled

Catalog	Disrepute	Maelstrom	Reprobate
Contravene	Fickle	Nonchalant	Simian
Delineate	Genial	Opulent	Solicitous
Deprecate	Haughty	Proficient	Strenuous
Deride	Inquisitive	Quandary	Undermine

Word Scramble #28

1. CIILOOSSTU   S _____
2. CEFIINOPRT   P _____
3. DEEIMNNRU   U _____
4. AACGLOT   C _____
5. ABEEOPRRT   R _____
6. DDEEIR   D _____
7. AIIMNS   S _____
8. AEGILN   G _____
9. ELNOPTU   O _____
10. CEFIKL   F _____
11. AADNQRUY   Q _____
12. ADEEEILNT   D _____
13. AGHHTUY   H _____
14. ACDEEEPRT   D _____
15. AELMMORST   M _____
16. ACEENNORTV   C _____
17. ENORSSTUU   S _____
18. EIIIINQSTUV   I _____
19. DEEIPRSTU   D _____
20. AACHLNNNOT   N _____

172

Word Search #28

```
P I N Q U I S I T I V E F Z
C H N G P Y W J Z O X V O C
A B D R X D E P R E C A T E
E Q P S O L I C I T O U S L
R E P R O B A T E H N E X L
O N U D E L I N E A T E V Y
L P O N Y X Q O N U R W V D
B R Q N D X E Q P G A A V V
C O U E C E P E S H V B N S
A F A T S H R A I T E I M V
P I N V A S A M M Y N D Y Y
B C D R I T G L I H E B G E
Y I A D G R C U A N S O Q T
D E R I D E Q U N N E G Z T
L N Y S L N N X E X T O E J
Z T N K G U W I B S C U E V
X N C V I O U C A T A L O G
Y I Y A L U O P U L E N T S
F M A E L S T R O M T F U O
B J M G D M J S X W F K V X
```

Crossword Clues #28

Across

3. Loss of good reputation
4. Concerned
6. Friendly
9. Changeable or unpredictable
10. A perplexed
12. Skilled
13. Apelike
15. To belittle
17. To contradict
18. Disdainfully proud

Down

1. Rich and superior in quality
2. A person without moral scruples
4. Requiring great effort
5. To describe
7. Curious
8. Weaken gradually or secretly
11. A violent commotion or disturbance
14. Having a lack of concern
15. To laugh at mockingly
16. To list

Crossword Puzzle #28

Word List #1 Solutions

Word List

1. Pious
2. Verbose
3. Discriminate
4. Bombastic
5. Tractable
6. Deplore
7. Acquiesce
8. Constrain
9. Exalt
10. Behemoth
11. Insurgent
12. Pertinacious
13. Replete
14. Slight
15. Antagonist
16. Convention
17. Timorous
18. Austere
19. Futile
20. Pedestrian

Word Scramble

1. Discriminate
2. Austere
3. Acquiesce
4. Behemoth
5. Slight
6. Futile
7. Antagonist
8. Verbose
9. Convention
10. Exalt
11. Timorous
12. Insurgent
13. Pertinacious
14. Constrain
15. Deplore
16. Replete
17. Pedestrian
18. Tractable
19. Pious
20. Bombastic

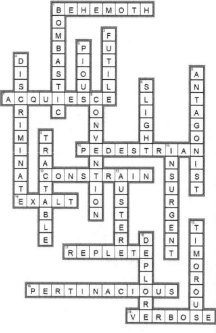

Word List #2 Solutions

Word List

1. Hypothetical
2. Virtue
3. Composure
4. Subside
5. Morass
6. Burnish
7. Taciturn
8. Guile
9. Petulance
10. Amiable
11. Wheedle
12. Cherish
13. Tryst
14. Consign
15. Recapitulate
16. Bourgeois
17. Quotidian
18. Wry
19. Artisan
20. Mitigate

Word Scramble

1. Petulance
2. Amiable
3. Cherish
4. Mitigate
5. Hypothetical
6. Wry
7. Artisan
8. Wheedle
9. Recapitulate
10. Burnish
11. Composure
12. Tryst
13. Consign
14. Bourgeois
15. Subside
16. Quotidian
17. Morass
18. Virtue
19. Guile
20. Taciturn

Word List #3 Solutions

Word List

1. Feasible
2. Incarnate
3. Dither
4. Respite
5. Depravity
6. Archetypal
7. Decorous
8. Luminous
9. Dormant
10. Enthrall
11. Indefatigable
12. Relegate
13. Reservoir
14. Assuage
15. Salve
16. Credulity
17. Apathetic
18. Expedite
19. Brevity
20. Collateral

Word Scramble

1. Reservoir
2. Enthrall
3. Brevity
4. Apathetic
5. Depravity
6. Dormant
7. Luminous
8. Feasible
9. Respite
10. Expedite
11. Incarnate
12. Dither
13. Archetypal
14. Collateral
15. Salve
16. Decorous
17. Assuage
18. Relegate
19. Credulity
20. Indefatigable

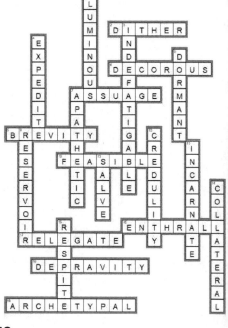

178

Word List #4 Solutions

Word List

1. Atrophy
2. Perspicacity
3. Potable
4. Remedial
5. Inept
6. Choreographed
7. Dynamic
8. Palatable
9. Buttress
10. Abhor
11. Lurid
12. Alacrity
13. Serendipity
14. Vehement
15. Antagonism
16. Peripheral
17. Amorphous
18. Ambivalent
19. Impertinent
20. Solitude

Word Scramble

1. Peripheral
2. Serendipity
3. Remedial
4. Inept
5. Choreographed
6. Palatable
7. Antagonism
8. Buttress
9. Alacrity
10. Perspicacity
11. Dynamic
12. Atrophy
13. Ambivalent
14. Solitude
15. Impertinent
16. Abhor
17. Amorphous
18. Lurid
19. Potable
20. Vehement

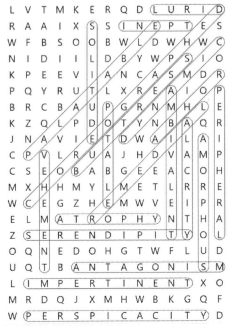

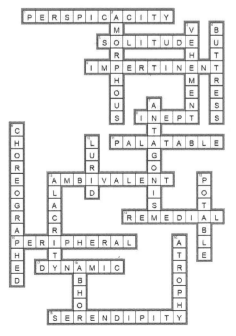

179

Word List #5 Solutions

Word List

1. Virtuoso
2. Incorrigible
3. Compensate
4. Nominal
5. Fracas
6. Dour
7. Engender
8. Transmute
9. Indomitable
10. Digress
11. Colossus
12. Flabbergasted
13. Latent
14. Appease
15. Affront
16. Indignant
17. Inexorable
18. Impervious
19. Apprehend
20. Abject

Word Scramble

1. Nominal
2. Engender
3. Indignant
4. Indomitable
5. Transmute
6. Inexorable
7. Colossus
8. Apprehend
9. Appease
10. Abject
11. Virtuoso
12. Latent
13. Digress
14. Flabbergasted
15. Fracas
16. Affront
17. Incorrigible
18. Impervious
19. Compensate
20. Dour

180

Word List #6 Solutions

Word List

1. Deference
2. Surly
3. Compliant
4. Celerity
5. Novice
6. Avarice
7. Accessible
8. Aspersion
9. Accentuate
10. Sagacious
11. Upbraid
12. Tenable
13. Plaudits
14. Wistful
15. Paradigm
16. Indigent
17. Idiosyncratic
18. Tentative
19. Saccharine
20. Approbation

Word Scramble

1. Accentuate
2. Compliant
3. Deference
4. Celerity
5. Sagacious
6. Indigent
7. Plaudits
8. Accessible
9. Wistful
10. Surly
11. Tenable
12. Aspersion
13. Approbation
14. Saccharine
15. Tentative
16. Upbraid
17. Idiosyncratic
18. Avarice
19. Novice
20. Paradigm

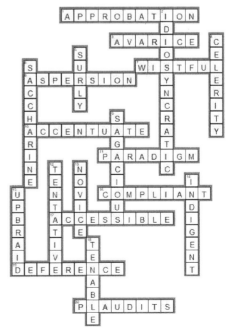

Word List #7 Solutions

Word List

1. Larceny
2. Staid
3. Apathy
4. Distend
5. Pungent
6. Inoculate
7. Ravenous
8. Animosity
9. Inchoate
10. Conspicuous
11. Resolution
12. Expedient
13. Vex
14. Iridescent
15. Accede
16. Impinge
17. Vilify
18. Tangential
19. Contemporaneous
20. Semaphore

Word Scramble

1. Distend
2. Impinge
3. Contemporaneous
4. Iridescent
5. Accede
6. Vilify
7. Inchoate
8. Tangential
9. Expedient
10. Resolution
11. Apathy
12. Semaphore
13. Vex
14. Conspicuous
15. Pungent
16. Staid
17. Larceny
18. Inoculate
19. Ravenous
20. Animosity

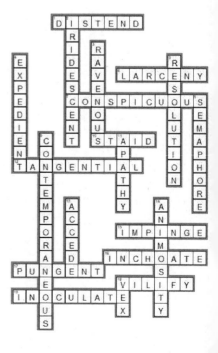

182

Word List #8 Solutions

Word List

1. Audible
2. Exorbitant
3. Dissipate
4. Precarious
5. Prosperity
6. Obtuse
7. Laud
8. Assess
9. Derivative
10. Amenable
11. Adorn
12. Acerbic
13. Contentious
14. Antipathy
15. Commendation
16. Pariah
17. Cerebral
18. Artifact
19. Indolence
20. Arbitration

Word Scramble

1. Commendation
2. Adorn
3. Assess
4. Contentious
5. Obtuse
6. Cerebral
7. Acerbic
8. Arbitration
9. Indolence
10. Artifact
11. Prosperity
12. Precarious
13. Dissipate
14. Laud
15. Antipathy
16. Audible
17. Derivative
18. Amenable
19. Pariah
20. Exorbitant

183

Word List #9 Solutions

Word List

1. Parched
2. Pulchritude
3. Zenith
4. Neophyte
5. Ardor
6. Regurgitate
7. Insular
8. Overcome
9. Meander
10. Consumption
11. Inferred
12. Abjure
13. Foil
14. Captivate
15. Debase
16. Substantiate
17. Melancholy
18. Bequeath
19. Arbiter
20. Endorse

Word Scramble

1. Substantiate
2. Arbiter
3. Neophyte
4. Debase
5. Captivate
6. Inferred
7. Meander
8. Ardor
9. Insular
10. Parched
11. Foil
12. Bequeath
13. Abjure
14. Endorse
15. Regurgitate
16. Consumption
17. Melancholy
18. Zenith
19. Pulchritude
20. Overcome

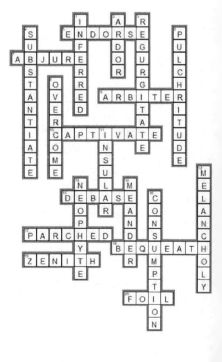

Word List #10 Solutions

Word List

1. Eclectic
2. Preponderance
3. Stagnant
4. Adumbrate
5. Alleviate
6. Subtle
7. Veracity
8. Sacrosanct
9. Profane
10. Clandestine
11. Redoubtable
12. Complicit
13. Arrogate
14. Incongruous
15. Bolster
16. Provincial
17. Ambiguous
18. Analogous
19. Lavish
20. Fatuous

Word Scramble

1. Profane
2. Ambiguous
3. Clandestine
4. Subtle
5. Adumbrate
6. Sacrosanct
7. Provincial
8. Redoubtable
9. Fatuous
10. Incongruous
11. Eclectic
12. Veracity
13. Lavish
14. Complicit
15. Bolster
16. Arrogate
17. Stagnant
18. Preponderance
19. Analogous
20. Alleviate

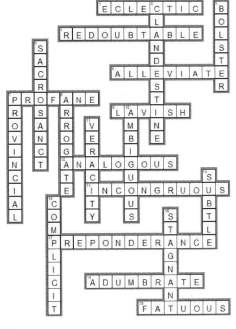

185

Word List #11 Solutions

1. Carouse
2. Expunge
3. Conceive
4. Verdant
5. Nostalgic
6. Subterfuge
7. Disparity
8. Integral
9. Grandiloquence
10. Prohibitively
11. Reprehensible
12. Disheartened
13. Domineering
14. Susceptible
15. Consolation
16. Flaccid
17. Rife
18. Penchant
19. Convivial
20. Blithe

1. Rife
2. Subterfuge
3. Convivial
4. Conceive
5. Susceptible
6. Disheartened
7. Nostalgic
8. Verdant
9. Disparity
10. Integral
11. Blithe
12. Reprehensible
13. Prohibitively
14. Penchant
15. Domineering
16. Expunge
17. Carouse
18. Grandiloquence
19. Consolation
20. Flaccid

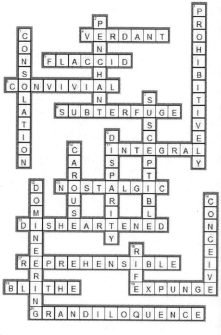

186

Word List #12 Solutions

Word List

1. Pious
2. Verbose
3. Discriminate
4. Bombastic
5. Tractable
6. Deplore
7. Acquiesce
8. Constrain
9. Exalt
10. Behemoth
11. Insurgent
12. Pertinacious
13. Replete
14. Slight
15. Antagonist
16. Convention
17. Timorous
18. Austere
19. Futile
20. Pedestrian

Word Scramble

1. Accord
2. Pretentious
3. Bonhomie
4. Chide
5. Benefactor
6. Philanthropy
7. Allege
8. Extricate
9. Winsome
10. Despondent
11. Ineffable
12. Articulate
13. Indulgent
14. Aggrieve
15. Transitory
16. Vacillate
17. Perfunctory
18. Effrontery
19. Cordial
20. Irascible

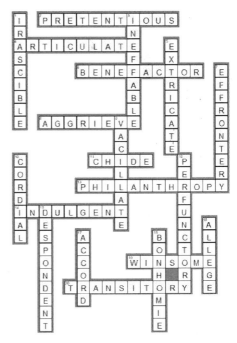

187

Word List #13 Solutions

Word List

1. Implacable
2. Truculent
3. Torrid
4. Anthology
5. Remiss
6. Paucity
7. Orthodox
8. Pivotal
9. Reputable
10. Callous
11. Contemporary
12. Indolent
13. Ebullient
14. Aversion
15. Submissive
16. Notorious
17. Uniform
18. Ingenuous
19. Panacea
20. Hallowed

Word Scramble

1. Anthology
2. Paucity
3. Panacea
4. Ingenuous
5. Callous
6. Implacable
7. Contemporary
8. Remiss
9. Submissive
10. Truculent
11. Reputable
12. Indolent
13. Orthodox
14. Pivotal
15. Torrid
16. Uniform
17. Ebullient
18. Hallowed
19. Notorious
20. Aversion

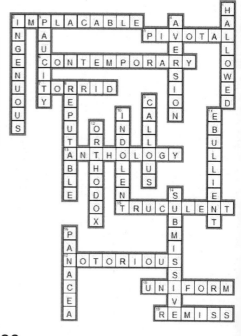

188

Word List #14 Solutions

Word List

1. Tortuous
2. Cloying
3. Rhapsodize
4. Lithe
5. Mnemonic
6. Nurture
7. Bane
8. Mores
9. Anesthesia
10. Sobriety
11. Multifarious
12. Temperance
13. Amass
14. Utopia
15. Deliberate
16. Negligent
17. Emollient
18. Inclined
19. Plenitude
20. Litigant

Word Scramble

1. Rhapsodize
2. Temperance
3. Cloying
4. Amass
5. Utopia
6. Deliberate
7. Mnemonic
8. Multifarious
9. Sobriety
10. Anesthesia
11. Plenitude
12. Negligent
13. Inclined
14. Nurture
15. Mores
16. Tortuous
17. Bane
18. Lithe
19. Litigant
20. Emollient

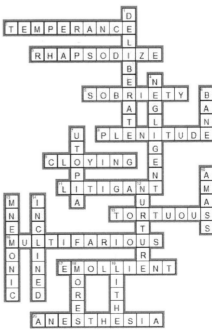

189

Word List #15 Solutions

Word List

1. Tome
2. Empirical
3. Astute
4. Immutable
5. Fortuitous
6. Resolute
7. Anathema
8. Camaraderie
9. Enfranchise
10. Consensus
11. Sapient
12. Covet
13. Congeal
14. Censor
15. Elegy
16. Valid
17. Platitude
18. Disclose
19. Divulge
20. Inveterate

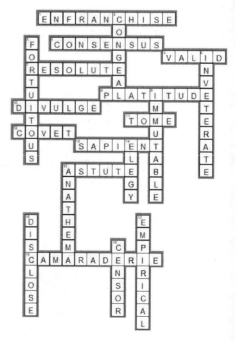

Word Scramble

1. Immutable
2. Tome
3. Sapient
4. Resolute
5. Camaraderie
6. Fortuitous
7. Divulge
8. Elegy
9. Platitude
10. Empirical
11. Censor
12. Astute
13. Disclose
14. Congeal
15. Enfranchise
16. Covet
17. Consensus
18. Inveterate
19. Valid
20. Anathema

Word List #16 Solutions

1. Pervasive
2. Inhibit
3. Arable
4. Clergy
5. Banal
6. Interject
7. Collusion
8. Jeopardy
9. Nomadic
10. Aloof
11. Emulate
12. Efface
13. Conundrum
14. Deplete
15. Impudent
16. Cosmopolitan
17. Pernicious
18. Succinct
19. Debauch
20. Bashful

1. Jeopardy
2. Aloof
3. Collusion
4. Interject
5. Pervasive
6. Conundrum
7. Deplete
8. Nomadic
9. Bashful
10. Clergy
11. Pernicious
12. Emulate
13. Debauch
14. Impudent
15. Efface
16. Inhibit
17. Cosmopolitan
18. Banal
19. Arable
20. Succinct

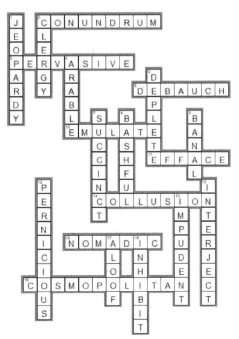

191

Word List #17 Solutions

Word List

1. Copious
2. Strain
3. Revere
4. Canvas
5. Anachronistic
6. Trepidation
7. Sovereign
8. Abate
9. Appalling
10. Inclination
11. Reiterate
12. Maxim
13. Deface
14. Reconcile
15. Ignominious
16. Caricature
17. Repose
18. Enhance
19. Metamorphosis
20. Adamant

Word Scramble

1. Inclination
2. Maxim
3. Metamorphosis
4. Reconcile
5. Copious
6. Ignominious
7. Repose
8. Caricature
9. Canvas
10. Sovereign
11. Revere
12. Strain
13. Abate
14. Enhance
15. Appalling
16. Trepidation
17. Adamant
18. Anachronistic
19. Reiterate
20. Deface

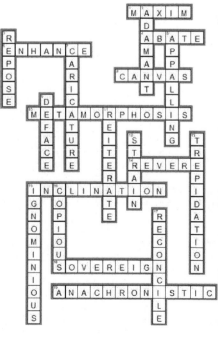

Word List #18 Solutions

Word List

1. Calibrate
2. Repudiate
3. Enigma
4. Insipid
5. Aggrandize
6. Audacious
7. Illicit
8. Augment
9. Complacency
10. Harrowing
11. Nocturnal
12. Inane
13. Debacle
14. Modulate
15. Canny
16. Retract
17. Parody
18. Desolate
19. Chronicle
20. Buffet

Word Scramble

1. Modulate
2. Canny
3. Complacency
4. Debacle
5. Buffet
6. Illicit
7. Desolate
8. Parody
9. Retract
10. Calibrate
11. Harrowing
12. Aggrandize
13. Augment
14. Inane
15. Audacious
16. Chronicle
17. Enigma
18. Insipid
19. Repudiate
20. Nocturnal

193

Word List #19 Solutions

Word List

1. Fervor
2. Mendacious
3. Juxtaposition
4. Propagate
5. Insolent
6. Immerse
7. Ameliorate
8. Ostentatious
9. Daunting
10. Contusion
11. Ingenious
12. Chronological
13. Duplicity
14. Primordial
15. Placate
16. Truncate
17. Maudlin
18. Ingratiate
19. Pugnacious
20. Ostensible

Word Scramble

1. Ameliorate
2. Maudlin
3. Ingenious
4. Fervor
5. Duplicity
6. Daunting
7. Ostentatious
8. Chronological
9. Truncate
10. Primordial
11. Mendacious
12. Insolent
13. Immerse
14. Ingratiate
15. Juxtaposition
16. Propagate
17. Contusion
18. Placate
19. Ostensible
20. Pugnacious

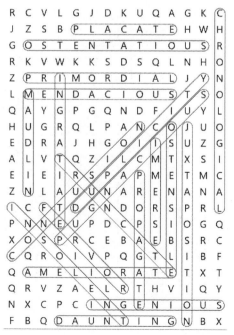

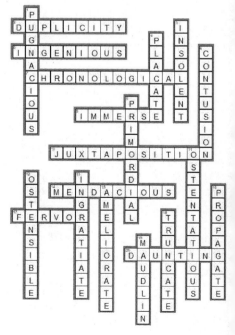

194

Word List #20 Solutions

Word List

1. Raze
2. Authentic
3. Affinity
4. Wallow
5. Neutral
6. Diverse
7. Ethereal
8. Hierarchy
9. Amicable
10. Erudite
11. Biased
12. Resignation
13. Didactic
14. Licentious
15. Effervescent
16. Palpable
17. Appraise
18. Counteract
19. Efficacious
20. Corrosive

Word Scramble

1. Resignation
2. Licentious
3. Ethereal
4. Palpable
5. Authentic
6. Appraise
7. Counteract
8. Didactic
9. Diverse
10. Raze
11. Hierarchy
12. Corrosive
13. Biased
14. Erudite
15. Affinity
16. Neutral
17. Efficacious
18. Effervescent
19. Amicable
20. Wallow

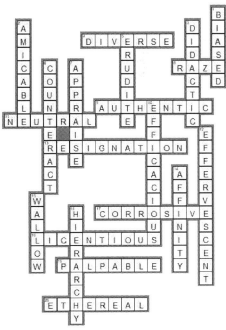

195

Word List #21 Solutions

Word List

1. Onerous
2. Objective
3. Balk
4. Diffident
5. Discern
6. Malevolent
7. Fanatic
8. Undulate
9. Gregarious
10. Stoic
11. Empathy
12. Abet
13. Abscond
14. Ennui
15. Advocate
16. Resolve
17. Incumbent
18. Capacious
19. Heresy
20. Elaborate

Word Scramble

1. Resolve
2. Objective
3. Heresy
4. Malevolent
5. Discern
6. Elaborate
7. Abet
8. Stoic
9. Advocate
10. Balk
11. Onerous
12. Diffident
13. Empathy
14. Gregarious
15. Ennui
16. Abscond
17. Undulate
18. Incumbent
19. Fanatic
20. Capacious

Word List #22 Solutions

Word List

1. Iconoclast
2. Hardy
3. Belittle
4. Morose
5. Garish
6. Quaint
7. Ironic
8. Intrinsic
9. Umbrage
10. Magnanimous
11. Vagrant
12. Cognizant
13. Tirade
14. Transient
15. Jocular
16. Gullible
17. Stringent
18. Denigrate
19. Propensity
20. Corroborate

Word Scramble

1. Cognizant
2. Gullible
3. Stringent
4. Tirade
5. Transient
6. Iconoclast
7. Corroborate
8. Ironic
9. Umbrage
10. Propensity
11. Intrinsic
12. Quaint
13. Belittle
14. Denigrate
15. Jocular
16. Vagrant
17. Hardy
18. Garish
19. Magnanimous
20. Morose

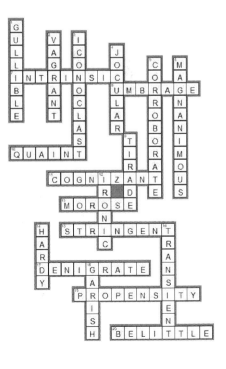

197

Word List #23 Solutions

Word List

1. Diminutive
2. Disparage
3. Obstreperous
4. Bilk
5. Itinerant
6. Restitution
7. Intrepid
8. Recalibrate
9. Discomfit
10. Defunct
11. Cunning
12. Dissent
13. Rancid
14. Mandate
15. Compatible
16. Antithesis
17. Precipice
18. Frivolous
19. Impassive
20. Animated

Word Scramble

1. Antithesis
2. Animated
3. Obstreperous
4. Diminutive
5. Rancid
6. Defunct
7. Precipice
8. Dissent
9. Recalibrate
10. Itinerant
11. Compatible
12. Disparage
13. Discomfit
14. Frivolous
15. Mandate
16. Restitution
17. Impassive
18. Intrepid
19. Bilk
20. Cunning

198

Word List #24 Solutions

Word List

1. Aspire
2. Subsidiary
3. Universal
4. Eccentric
5. Fervent
6. Defer
7. Submerge
8. Reactionary
9. Antiquated
10. Manifold
11. Refute
12. Anecdote
13. Infamy
14. Atone
15. Coherent
16. Prevalent
17. Adroit
18. Debunk
19. Subjugate
20. Arcane

Word Scramble

1. Infamy
2. Fervent
3. Manifold
4. Anecdote
5. Arcane
6. Subjugate
7. Coherent
8. Defer
9. Universal
10. Prevalent
11. Aspire
12. Submerge
13. Debunk
14. Eccentric
15. Subsidiary
16. Antiquated
17. Reactionary
18. Atone
19. Adroit
20. Refute

Word List #25 Solutions

Word List

1. Admonish
2. Trivial
3. Paltry
4. Nebulous
5. Virulent
6. Eloquent
7. Arrogant
8. Epitome
9. Invective
10. Miser
11. Rescind
12. Erratic
13. Agile
14. Accolade
15. Abrogate
16. Reticent
17. Uncanny
18. Amity
19. Zealous
20. Prudent

Word Scramble

1. Amity
2. Virulent
3. Eloquent
4. Agile
5. Trivial
6. Invective
7. Zealous
8. Paltry
9. Erratic
10. Accolade
11. Epitome
12. Admonish
13. Prudent
14. Rescind
15. Nebulous
16. Abrogate
17. Reticent
18. Miser
19. Arrogant
20. Uncanny

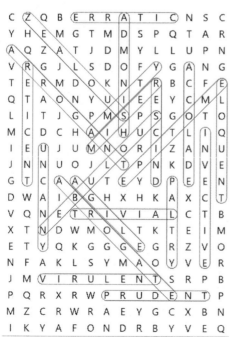

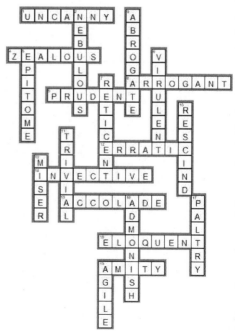

Word List #26 Solutions

Word List

1. Candid
2. Whet
3. Obtrusive
4. Strife
5. Exuberant
6. Proscribe
7. Ascetic
8. Fecund
9. Obfuscate
10. Acute
11. Sensuous
12. Reclusive
13. Condone
14. Convene
15. Abdicate
16. Acumen
17. Fathom
18. Protean
19. Affluent
20. Brusque

Word Scramble

1. Ascetic
2. Protean
3. Condone
4. Affluent
5. Abdicate
6. Convene
7. Sensuous
8. Fathom
9. Proscribe
10. Whet
11. Acute
12. Fecund
13. Candid
14. Acumen
15. Obfuscate
16. Obtrusive
17. Reclusive
18. Exuberant
19. Brusque
20. Strife

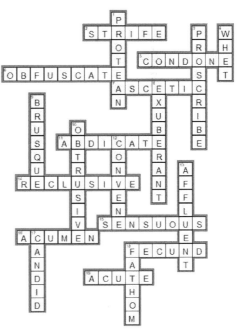

Word List #27 Solutions

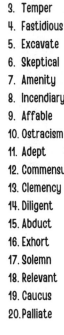

Word List

1. Affable
2. Clemency
3. Ostracism
4. Solemn
5. Incendiary
6. Relevant
7. Diligent
8. Adept
9. Amenity
10. Nascent
11. Temper
12. Abduct
13. Fastidious
14. Exhort
15. Commensurate
16. Excavate
17. Skeptical
18. Palliate
19. Caucus
20. Effulgent

Word Scramble

1. Effulgent
2. Nascent
3. Temper
4. Fastidious
5. Excavate
6. Skeptical
7. Amenity
8. Incendiary
9. Affable
10. Ostracism
11. Adept
12. Commensurate
13. Clemency
14. Diligent
15. Abduct
16. Exhort
17. Solemn
18. Relevant
19. Caucus
20. Palliate

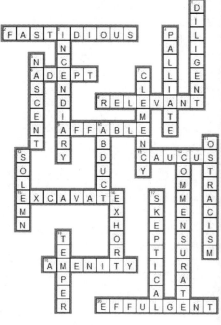

Word List #28 Solutions

Word List

1. Deride
2. Deprecate
3. Quandary
4. Undermine
5. Reprobate
6. Nonchalant
7. Genial
8. Catalog
9. Solicitous
10. Maelstrom
11. Inquisitive
12. Fickle
13. Opulent
14. Simian
15. Haughty
16. Disrepute
17. Strenuous
18. Delineate
19. Contravene
20. Proficient

Word Scramble

1. Solicitous
2. Proficient
3. Undermine
4. Catalog
5. Reprobate
6. Deride
7. Simian
8. Genial
9. Opulent
10. Fickle
11. Quandary
12. Delineate
13. Haughty
14. Deprecate
15. Maelstrom
16. Contravene
17. Strenuous
18. Inquisitive
19. Disrepute
20. Nonchalant

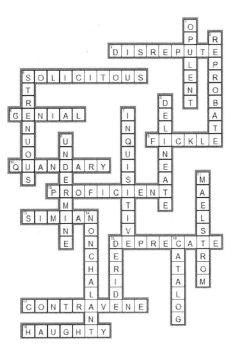

203

References & Resources

To further assist you in your SAT & ACT preparation, we've compiled a list of valuable resources. These websites offer a variety of tools and information to help you expand your vocabulary and enhance your overall test performance.

Resource	Description	QR code
Vocabulary.com	A great tool for learning new words and their meanings through interactive activities and quizzes.	
Dictionary.com	An extensive online dictionary providing definitions, synonyms, and more.	
College Board SAT	Official SAT practice resources, including sample questions, practice tests, and study guides.	
ACT	The official ACT website provides test information, study tips, and practice questions.	
Khan Academy	Free, personalized SAT practice with video lessons, practice questions, and full-length tests.	

References & Resources

Resource	Description	QR code
Prep Scholar	Offers comprehensive SAT and ACT prep courses, practice tests, and tips for improving your scores.	
Merriam-Webster	A trusted dictionary and thesaurus with word games and vocabulary quizzes.	
Quizlet	A platform to create and study custom flashcards, and access pre-made sets for SAT and ACT vocabulary.	
The Princeton Review	Offers test prep courses, practice tests, and study materials for the SAT and ACT.	
Kaplan Test Prep	Provides SAT and ACT prep courses, practice tests, and personalized study plans.	
Number2	Free online SAT and ACT test prep, including vocabulary building tools and practice questions.	
ETS (Educational Testing Service)	Offers information and practice materials for various standardized tests, including the SAT and ACT.	

Be Our Hero

Help us stamp out cancer, protect animals, empower children, eradicate hunger, and make the world a better place. We will donate 50% of the proceeds for June 2024 and 10% of the proceeds in subsequent months to the charity with the most votes. Please use the QR code below to cast your vote from the list of charities, check current charity rankings, and view donation amounts.

Dear Reader,

Thank you for choosing the "SAT & ACT Vocabulary Workbook #1"! We hope you had fun learning new words and feel more prepared for your SAT or ACT test. If you found this workbook helpful, please consider leaving a review. Your feedback helps others discover this resource and supports your selected charity.

Thank you for your support!

Archana & Maya

Made in the USA
Columbia, SC
29 June 2025

60104703R00113